Kill Mom

Bob Bradley

TABLE OF CONTENTS

I walked into my sister's kitchen, obviously upset. Pat asked, "What's wrong?"

"Our new 'Mom' wants me to show her how to program the cell phone Dad just bought her."

"So what's wrong with that?"

"Well, anyone who can figure out how to give an 85 year old man a blow job should be able to figure out how to program a cell phone!"

"Bob! You're talking about our father!"

"You're damned right I'm talking about our father!"

I

I first heard the name Carolyn Smith in July, 2000. Pat, my brother Bruce and I decided to throw a birthday party for our father Frank on his 85th Birthday in August, 2000, 9 months after our mother passed away. We would use the occasion in San Diego, where Pat and Dad lived 5 minutes from each other, to let him know how much we loved him and we would always be there to support him.

Dad had accepted our mother Mae's death and moved on, so to speak. He was always a very pragmatic, almost too-logical person. He had been a devoted husband for almost 60 years. She died, he grieved for a short period.......it was time to accept it and move on with his life.

When I called Pat from my home in Chicago to discuss the details of the week-long birthday celebration, Pat told me Dad had a new "squeeze" and he was definitely smitten. "What happened to Helen," who Dad had been dating for 3 months?

"Helen's history. Dad's ga-ga over Carolyn."

"That's great. I was really worried Dad would be in a funk and wouldn't get out of his house."

"Don't worry, our father is a long, long way from a funk. Carolyn's living at Dad's house and he's doing just fine."

"Wow! She's living up at his house? That was fast. How did they meet?"

"They met on the Internet, 'AOL In Love.' He saw her picture, met her for lunch at the Del Coronado Hotel, drove back to show her his house over-looking San Diego Bay and that was it. She spent the first night in the guest bedroom and graduated to the big bed with Dad the next night! She's been there ever since."

I was a little surprised but over-all happy Dad had found someone. He was not the type to go down to one of the retirement groups who meet at the Yacht Club every morning. We tried that but he wasn't interested. He needed someone to replace Mom. We knew he needed a woman in his life, he would probably get married again. I hoped it would be Helen, a wonderful, decent person who really cared about Dad. She would have made a great new companion for Dad.

What a relief. At least Dad would be happy so I wouldn't be living in Chicago, worrying about how lonely he was.

Dad had been a wonderful father, a hero to me. He was someone I could only admire, never emulate. He was too successful, too smart, too everything. He seemed to glide through life, achieving remarkable success with out giving the appearance of expending much effort. A college track scholarship because he had no money, colonel-on-his-way to general after 22 years in the Army, abrupt career change to Martin Marietta which ended with him on the Board of Directors in what is now Lockheed Martin.

He never lost his cool. I rarely saw him angry, never heard him use the F-word. Until he made a few typos when he started using a personal computer in his 70's, I never saw him misspell a word. Plus, everyone liked and admired Dad. Besides his amazing talent and ability, he was just a good guy who could relate and interact with anyone on any level. He was completely honest, assumed everyone else was, too.

Even though he had been in the Army until he was 43, he insisted everyone—-even other kids, his grandkids and bartenders at the

Yacht Club—-call him "Frank." He didn't need "Mister, Sir, Colonel." His record spoke for itself. Everyone knew how good he was.

What a man! What a scholar-athlete! He scrimmaged with Bear Bryant and Don Hudson at the University of Alabama in the mid-30's even though he was there on a track scholarship. Played football in the Army, was the star running back in a huge inter-service game before WWII. He cruised through Columbia for his masters thanks to the Army. He was faster than my twin and I when we were in high school, could out ice-skate us, could out-anything us. He was just good......and smart. One of his Army War College classmates said Dad had the best mind of anyone he'd been around. A man's man with a resume to prove it.

When Jess Sweetser retired from Martin Marietta, he said one of the highlights of his career was hiring Dad. Jess saw a lot in his life and had been around lots of Super Stars and celebrities. He beat Bobby Jones 8 and 7 in the U.S. Amateur Golf Tournament before Jones won the Grand Slam and, like Jones, won the U.S. and British Amateur titles. For good measure, Jess also won an NCAA Golf championship. All the top military brass including the Joint Chiefs of Staff wanted to play golf with Jess, which was great for Martin Marietta government defense business. Dad hated golf.

Dad loved the Army, planned to make it his career for at least 30 years. He had a superb record: Lieutenant Colonel at 30, Special Assistant to the Secretary of the Army, Assistant in the Army Chief of Staff's office, attended the Army War College. All his tickets were punched for an excellent shot at stars.

However, there was one thing missing in Dad's Army resume: combat. During WWII he was stationed in Panama, which was considered a critical assignment. Dad volunteered for combat and was preparing to move a Battalion to Europe when the war ended.

During the Korean War he was in the Chief of Staff's Office as an assistant to General Lawton Collins.

Even though he was in the Coast Artillery during WWII and the Infantry during the Korean War with out seeing combat, Dad had powerful mentors who assured him there were stars in his future. One was Ben Harrell who went on to four stars himself. Dad was not afraid of competition, always surrounding himself with very capable officers, including Fred Weyand, who went on to became Army Chief of Staff. Dad brought Weyand into the Secretary of the Army's office when they were Colonels.

Jess Sweetser, a Martin Marietta V.P., had heard about Dad from a fellow Martin Marietta employee who served in the Army with Dad in the early 1940's while stationed in Panama.

Dad turned down Jess' first job offer but Jess wouldn't take "no." A year later Jess flew to Fort Benning. Jess reminded Dad he still had time for a second twenty-year career at Martin Marietta, that Dad would be considered for general in a few years but his lack of combat experience might hurt his chances for stars. Dad needed to make a move now. In two or three years he might be considered too old for a career change.

Surprisingly, Dad decided to retire from the Army and join Martin Marietta. He was starting over at age 43, had no business experience, $2,000 to his name, three kids within three years of college and a salary of $13,000/year. Ten years later he lived in Brentwood, across from movie stars and not far from where O.J. eventually moved. Dad ended up on the Board of Directors of Martin Marietta and President of the most profitable Division.

We could only watch, admire. No way his kids were in his league. We knew it. Dad knew it, but never said so.

We were just happy he was "Dad." No spankings when we were young. He was too smart. He'd make you feel worse with words than any belt could.

And pragmatic. He got emotional when we took Mom's ashes up to Rosecrans National Cemetery at the top of Point Loma, but almost no tears. It was part of life, and all lives end in death. He had nothing to be ashamed about. He had done his job as a husband for 59 years. Accept the event, grieve, move on. No prolonged grieving, sniveling. That was for normal men. He was too analytical, too practical to get bogged down by something that might cripple the average man for weeks, months. Nothing more he could do. Move on.

I was thrilled Dad had someone in his life. The fact Carolyn had come off the Internet was no big deal to me. It was 2000 and things were different. His happiness was the only thing that mattered.

Since I was always the master of ceremonies at family gatherings, I had to get ready for his 85th Birthday Party at the San Diego Yacht Club. There would be over 50 people, mostly Pat's friends who had become Mae and Frank's friends once they retired to San Diego from Washington, D.C. in 1984. Most of Mae and Frank's friends had already passed on or couldn't travel.

My brother Bruce and I planned to stay in San Diego for an entire week. We made that decision before Carolyn came off the Internet because we thought Dad might be lonely and maybe we could help him get his life together.....if necessary. He had enjoyed being around Helen, who I hoped Dad would marry, but she wouldn't replace Mom.

Carolyn Smith could. I met Carolyn the first night I arrived in San Diego for the Birthday Week Celebration. Pat was having dinner at her house for 10 people and Carolyn was holding court in Pat's great room over-looking San Diego Yacht Club as I walked in.

What a charmer! At 68, 17 years younger than Dad and only ten years older than me, she looked like she was 55 at most. Charismatic, the master of ceremonies of any group, attractive; Carolyn was too good to be true. Dad had really found a winner. No surprise, though, he was used to being around winners.

Carolyn lived 45 minutes north of Point Loma at the "Lake." She had been in Southern California since the early 70's. Got married too young off a farm in Indiana, made a "mistake" with husband #1. Came out to California to start over, fell in love, married #2, Fred Smith. Realized Fred was an 'alcoholic mistake,' divorced him when Carolyn was 51....some 17 years earlier.

Carolyn loved people. She worked as a minimum-wage "volunteer" at a high-end retirement home near the Lake, escorted well-to-do elderly ladies to Europe when they needed someone to push their wheel chairs. Carolyn said she didn't need the money, she just liked helping people. Her "favorite time" was when she was in the kitchen, cooking for everyone; she wanted to spend Christmas with friends and relatives in Idelwild, near Palm Springs. Carolyn said life was all about family and friends

Carolyn controlled the conversation in any group. Not funny or witty, she could add semi-interesting bits and pieces to any conversation. She directed the discussion, usually about family values, home, cooking, helping at the retirement home, wanting marriage, blah, blah, blah.

And she couldn't give Dad too much attention. "Bradley, where are you taking me for lunch? Let's walk on the beach afterwards and pretend we're young."

"Your father is drop-dead gorgeous! He's the most handsome man I've ever met....at any age!" At Del Mar Race Track, "Frank, would you go down and ask that woman if she can get us better seats?" Turning to Pat, "Your father can charm the pants off any woman."

Whenever one of us kids was around Dad and Carolyn, Carolyn would always shower him with hugs, kisses and "isn't he just the most wonderful man!"

Not hard to believe, Dad was in heaven. We were beginning to think he had forgotten Mom's name. Of course, Mom may not have been giving him the sexual attention Carolyn was. Dad was amazing. He was going through industrial-strength Viagra like they were M&M's. When Pat took Dad to the Doctor, Dad would always ask to have his Viagra prescription re-filled. My worst fears were being realized: Dad was getting laid more than his kids!

Carolyn's shtick started unraveling about the 3d or 4th day. Her time-lines didn't make sense. She had been single for 17 years and now, all of a sudden, she was announcing to anyone she just had to get married. Couldn't get married fast enough.

She began contradicting earlier statements. Carolyn was taking a cruise with "Dutch" in a few months and had other boyfriends, so why was she looking for more men on the internet if she was so deliriously happy with a bunch of current admirers?

The more I was around Carolyn, the phonier she appeared. Everything was just too perfect. Here was this 68 year-old woman who seemed to have no baggage, no problems, no trouble cutting ties with her previous life. She was ready to move to Point Loma on a moments notice, forget the previous 68 years?

There were too many holes in her story. Too many things just didn't make sense. Was she, in fact, too good to be true?

The next-to-the-last night Carolyn was holding court once again in Pat's great room. Now, after five days of lunches and dinners, her performance seemed so scripted, like it was actually part of a performance. How many times had she acted in this play before? I was determined to find out.

Dad's 85th Birthday Party at the Yacht Club was a great time. I was "on" as master of ceremonies, gave Dad an actual Toyota bumper from Hawley Auto-Body—-where he had provided a lot of business—-with "Crash" as a personalized license plate to remind everyone what a horrible driver—-at any age—-Dad had been. While driving, he was the "Absent-Minded Professor." He was always thinking about big deals or something else, not driving, which led to numerous near-death experiences for the family.

When we were teenagers he decided to show us Manhattan, his home town. On one street the other drivers were beeping at us, making obscene gestures. Dad said, "You know, I grew up in New York but I've forgotten just how rude and obnoxious New York drivers are!"

I yelled, "Dad, that's because we're going down a one-way street the wrong way!"

Surprisingly, Dad paid tribute to our real Mother Mae while Carolyn was sitting next to him at his birthday party. Carolyn had a wry smirk on her face, which seemed to indicate "a couple more professional-strength blow jobs and this old man won't even remember what's-her-name's name." Carolyn knew what it took to win over a lonely seniors popping-Viagra. Carolyn had worked at Limp-Dick Retirement Home long enough to figure that out.

The last night of the Birthday week Dad took everyone who was still in San Diego—-9 of us—-to the Kaiserhof German restaurant in Point Loma. As desert was being served, Dad looked at Bruce, Pat and me and said, "I'd like to talk to you in the other room." I knew what he was going to say.

"You know I loved your mother very much. We were married almost 60 years. She was a wonderful woman. I'm 85 and don't know how much longer I have. With your approval, I'd like to marry Carolyn."

Pat burst out crying. In less than two months she had already developed an intense dislike for Carolyn. "Dad, what's the hurry?" Pat sobbed.

"Carolyn has a lot of suitors."

It was obvious Carolyn was putting tremendous pressure on Dad to step up to the marriage plate or she'd move on to Dutch, Ed, Henry, whomever. She wanted marriage now. She wanted Dad!

Dad, who had always been successful in life, was not about to let some average Joe win Carolyn. The Alpha Male wasn't used to coming in second and, at 85 with lots of money, wasn't about to start.

Even though Pat was very upset, I knew—-at this point—-it was not the time to debate the issue.

"Dad, the most important thing is your happiness. That's what I want." Bruce echoed my comments while Pat continued to sob. Pat lived within walking distance of Dad's house. She was not looking forward to life with Carolyn, who I derisively started calling "Mom" to Pat. I had already made up my mind several nights earlier I was going to find out who Carolyn Smith was. No one knew her. This stranger, who had come off the Internet seven weeks previously, was about to replace real Mom.

I didn't know much about Dad's finances but I heard our "Real" Mom say something about $10 million several years earlier. I knew their Point Loma house was worth at least $3 Million. President-Elect Richard Nixon tried to make it the Western White House but was forced to accept a San Clemente address when the Point Loma owner refused to sell or the Secret Service had security concerns. Two years after Nixon resigned the presidency, the owner of the house needed money so Mom and Dad bought the "almost-Western-White-House."

Dad informed us he would give Carolyn a "life estate" on his house. I didn't know what that meant. "Well, when I die, Carolyn's got to have a place to live." Obviously, Carolyn knew more about estate planning than we did.

I started making phone calls after returning home to Chicago, where I worked for a large packaging company. Carolyn said she had worked in real estate sales so I asked a friend's sister living at the Lake to see what she could find out.

A San Diego lawyer friend had used a private investigator; could my Pal recommend someone?

I mailed Private Investigator Howard a $1,000 retainer and signed some type of hourly agreement.

Almost immediately I heard from my friend's sister at the Lake. Her first phone call had been—-unbelievably—-to one of Carolyn's prior bosses, someone who owned a small real estate agency at the Lake. His response: "Tell your friends their father is engaged to the biggest gold digger in Southern California!"

I called Carolyn's ex-boss. To my surprise, he agreed to talk to me about Carolyn only if I did not use his name.

"Why? She's a 68 year-old woman!"

"Carolyn's not a nice person. She's dangerous and can be violent. Do not use my name; I'm very serious!"

It would not be the last time I heard that statement.

Carolyn's ex-boss continued, "Everyone here at the Lake knows about her. She preys on wealthy widowers and people at the retirement home. I had the displeasure of working with her. She is just one nasty, devious individual. A lot of people around here are afraid of Carolyn, including me."

My private eye Howard called a few days later. Bingo! Seems Carolyn forgot at least one marriage, several DUI's and an assault conviction against an 83 year old man named Larry. Carolyn had been married three times, but she had a total of seven names associated with her social security number. Howard also talked to Carolyn's last two husbands, the one she first married when she came to California—-Fred—-and Tim, who Carolyn met through the newspaper personals four years earlier, before she went high-tech on "AOL In Love."

Her old boss was right. Carolyn was not nice, especially to her spouses. Detective Howard said it was okay to call Fred and Tim....... they were eager to talk to me.

No kidding! I couldn't get them to stop talking. Carolyn was just a money-hungry, nasty Bitch: devious, dishonest, dangerous.

The only "compliments" I heard were "she is a good con artist" and "she's a charming opportunist." Everything else was negative.

Tim, 74, who met Carolyn through the Union Tribune personals four years previously, realized he had been pressured into marriage by Carolyn & filed for divorce immediately. Carolyn dragged out the divorce as long as she could because Tim, immediately after their marriage, was diagnosed with prostate cancer and Carolyn thought she could cash in if Tim died while they were still married. Tim had also lost his wife shortly before he met Carolyn and, like Dad, was elderly, lonely and, most importantly, well-off financially.

At one point Tim had to be talked out of killing Carolyn since he believed he was terminal. He thought, "When you've got nothing to lose" since he would be dead from prostate cancer shortly anyway. Tim's cancer was successfully treated and Carolyn finally agreed to a divorce after two years when Tim ponied up some money and promised to list his house sale with Carolyn. Tim wanted out of the Lake community, away from Carolyn.

Tim asked, "How old is your father?"

"85"

"Oh, she'll kill him within 6 months."

"What are you talking about? How would she do that?"

"Well, you mentioned your father is on anti-seizure medicine since he was diagnosed with epilepsy at 75 and had a stroke at 81. Carolyn will just replace his anti-seizure pills with a placebo and watch your father die after she switches over all his assets to her."

"I'm not sure she can do that. My understanding is there are trusts and stuff like that."

"It won't stop Carolyn. She's a crook. Trusts and prenups are for honest people. She's had a 15-year romantic relationship with a retired judge who's helped her get assets from people. She'll want your father to sell his house—-'too many memories'—-and buy another house in her name.....out of the area so she can isolate your father from you kids. She tried the same thing with me."

"Please, let me talk to your father so I can tell him what he's getting into."

Fred, 71, echoed Tim. Carolyn had cheated him out of half of his inheritance using a secret PO Box at the local Post Office—-and her son Dick and Love Judge Len Turner—-to forge documents.

Fred also made a huge mistake. Carolyn, a big drinker, fell off their boat several times at the Lake. Instead of helping an inebriated

Carolyn back on the boat, Fred said he should have put his foot on her head. I would eventually second that motion.

What a nice person. Carolyn's last two husbands openly talked about killing her.

Lovely! Our new Mom would be a great addition to the family. Only problem: Carolyn doesn't play well with husbands........hers!

Our Detective also located June, the niece of a retired wealthy banker who Carolyn almost got to the altar. The banker was completely insensitive to Carolyn's needs. He croaked before she could get him to the altar, although Carolyn was able to wring some money out of him, including money she needed to pay for a DUI. Almost everyone at the Lake was aware of the story, knew the banker "escaped" Carolyn's web.

I called June in up-state New York. She was very cooperative, helpful.

"My Uncle's bank called me, requesting information about a woman—-Carolyn Smith—-who showed up at the bank after my Uncle died. Carolyn claimed my Uncle had given his new Lincoln to her and she wanted the car. The bank wanted to know if I knew anything about it. I had had never heard the name 'Carolyn Smith.'

When I flew out to California to settle the estate, it was apparent my Uncle had given Carolyn thousands of dollars because, as a banker, he kept unbelievably accurate expense records.

I talked to some of the people at the Lake and it was obvious Carolyn was the local Gold Digger, preying on wealthy elderly men. Since my Uncle had been recently widowed, he was a choice target of opportunity.

I told the bank to forget Carolyn; she didn't deserve the car or anything else. From what I understood from the locals, Carolyn was very close to convincing my Uncle to marry her. Once my Uncle died, Carolyn just went on to her next victim, some guy named Erv."

Now what? Dad was going to marry Carolyn, but when? The one-year anniversary of real Mom's death was 2 months away, so I thought Dad would at least wait until then....or possibly Christmas-New Year, which was 4 months away. I knew, based on what I heard from Tim, Fred and Carolyn's old Real Estate Boss, Carolyn would keep the pressure on. My guess was they would get married in two months.....or sooner!

I had to be careful. If Dad discovered we were working behind the scenes to dig up dirt on Carolyn, he would immediately marry her.....to put a stop to any childish nonsense from his kids. Dad had found his fun and wouldn't let anyone, especially his own kids, spoil it. Dad obviously felt he was a good judge of people. He didn't get on the board of a Fortune 500 Company by accident.

I told Pat not to mention anything about my actions to my twin Bruce, who I didn't trust and was very unpredictable. Bruce just might tell Dad what I was doing. Why? Who knows? Bruce always wanted to be the key part of what was going on in the family and demanded attention. He might feel Pat and I were getting too much attention or, more likely, Bruce could get "extra credit" from Dad by warning him we were checking into Carolyn's background and motives. It was impossible to predict what Bruce might do, but it would be off-the-wall and damaging. That was his standard M.O.

Bruce called a couple days later to say, based on his wife Terri's revelation, he had a concern whether "Carolyn was on the up and up." Both he and Terri now felt Carolyn was a Scam Artist interested only in Dad's money.

I praised Bruce and told him I had my own suspicions, but would now check into Carolyn's background seriously......thanks to his "heads up."

You always had to kiss Bruce's ass to make him feel important or he'd do something to get attention that could really be damaging. Family politics are so much fun!

I began formulating a plan. Thanks to promised help from Tim, Fred and Carolyn's ex-boss, I would interview as many people as possible by phone, compile a dossier on Carolyn, and then Bruce, who lived in Washington, D.C., and I would fly to San Diego. We would some how get Dad alone to present our case against Carolyn. Even if Dad rejected our evidence, Carolyn would surely beat a path out of Dad's life once she learned we had uncovered her sordid past and motive.

During this time a lawyer warned me, even if Dad agreed to boot Carolyn out of his house, she did not have to leave for 72 hours. What! Yep, we had to give Carolyn a "reasonable" amount of time to arrange living accommodations since she had been invited into Dad's house. I explained Carolyn had her own townhouse. Didn't matter, she still had 72 hours according to the law.

Wonderful! So I spent a considerable amount of time making security arrangements [including me probably sleeping at Dad's] in case Carolyn demanded her full 72 hours. Since she had worked in Real Estate, maybe she knew the law.

Fred and Tim both lived near Carolyn at the Lake, a close-knit retirement community. They knew all Carolyn's neighbors and where the closet skeletons were located......and Carolyn had a bunch: the Retired Banker who died before Carolyn could get him to the altar, but she still tried to convince his bank that his new Lincoln was hers; an elderly woman—-Geraldine—-Carolyn had met at the retirement home. Carolyn got herself appointed executor of the woman's estate, depleting the assets and ending up owning the woman's town home. There were also rumors that Carolyn, also as conservator, stuck Geraldine—-who had Alzheimer's—-in an un-heated back bedroom until she died from neglect. Carolyn then quickly had her victim cremated.

Six neighbors, mostly men, all said the same thing about Carolyn: "Dangerous, violent, Gold Digger; do not use my name. Do *ANYTHING* to keep your father from marrying her!"

I remembered Dad saying [with Carolyn beaming beside him], "I'll be proud to have Carolyn on my arm during 'Honors Night' at the Lockheed-Martin annual shareholder's meeting [which included retired Directors]." Carolyn at anything associated with "Honors?" It would be like inviting Bill Clinton to a Celebration of Virgins.

In the end I talked to 14 people: neighbors, ex-husbands & bosses, victims. They were unanimous: unless you don't like your father, Carolyn is not someone you want around Dad. She would not be good for his health, especially after she got control of his assets. Carolyn was not interested in watching Dad grow old gracefully. She was ruthless, interested only in money. Carolyn was almost 69 and wanted money now!

I had yet to find even one person who had anything good to say about Carolyn.

Bruce had his best friend, an Ex-CIA guy, pull up Carolyn's police records, which included the assault conviction against Larry, an 83 year-old, and a couple DUI convictions. Bruce's friend: "Get your Dad some track shoes so he can get away from her as fast as possible!"

I called Larry, who met Carolyn through the newspaper. He confirmed Carolyn "is cold-blooded, interested only in money. She's rough and dangerous; do not tell her you talked to me!"

Whenever I called Dad, he'd always put Carolyn on the phone. It was important we got to know and accept our new family member. She continually showered us with false praise in an effort to win our hearts and minds while I continually pretended to like the phony Bitch.

Carolyn repeatedly told us she was very happy, had "finally found the man she wanted to spend the rest of her life with."

In the meantime I pursued my efforts to find out more about "Mom." It would take a lot of evidence to convince Dad that Carolyn was not someone he should spend the rest of his life with. Would any amount of "proof" be enough?

Bruce and I told Dad it was a coincidence we would be in California at the same time, about 4 weeks after Dad's big birthday party. Carolyn became suspicious, wanting to know why Bruce and I were coming back to California so soon. Not knowing anything about our activities and trusting us, Dad convinced Carolyn there was nothing to worry about. We were good kids and, besides, Dad was in control of everything. He was still C.E.O. of the family.

It would be a tough sell. Dad would not give up his new sex toy easily. He was deliriously happy. Someone was paying serious attention to making him happy for probably the first time in decades. Not that Real Mom didn't love Dad, but there's no way she had been servicing Dad to the extent Carolyn was. Real Mom didn't have to. She already shared the assets.

It was surprising how much input both of Carolyn's ex-husbands wanted to provide us. I never talked to her first husband from Indiana, but #2 and #3 made no secret of how much they despised Carolyn. They both agreed to meet with us at Pat's house the night before we confronted Dad in order to provide us as much ammunition against Carolyn as possible. Bruce and I had flown in that day, with Bruce staying up at Dad's house and me at Pat's.

Tim was a retired Navy Chief who had also retired with a nice pension from Scripts Hospital. I was impressed by his pride in his Navy service and his honesty. It was also obvious how easily Carolyn could have duped him into marriage. Tim had been warned by many of his friends that Carolyn didn't seem to be legit, but Tim was very lonely after losing his wife several months previously. He resorted to newspaper personals to find companionship, locating Carolyn. Carolyn finally gave him an ultimatum, so they flew to Vegas on short notice and got married. Carolyn got drunk, passed out. Forget sex; Tim never touched her again. Over-night, Carolyn turned into a first class Bitch. Tim realized during the first week of marriage he'd been conned, that their relationship was about Carolyn getting money—-Tim's!

Tim had on-going heart problems. After being married to Carolyn a few months, Tim's heart doctor demanded to know what had changed in Tim's life. "Whatever you're doing now, you MUST stop it or it will kill you." Without knowing it, the doctor was of course talking about the lovely Miss Carolyn.

Tim wasn't bitter. He actually complimented Carolyn, saying she was a good con artist and Tim deserved his fate for being so gullible, ignoring warnings from his many friends. No outward hatred, just facts: "She'll kill your father within 6 months."

"Someone with nothing to lose will kill her." Tim seemed glad he decided not to do it himself, that his new wife Susan—-who he met at work—-talked him out of it. Had Tim's prostate cancer been confirmed as terminal, it was obvious he would have killed Carolyn.

Fred was a different story. Fred wasn't very smart. He sold real estate at the Lake and married Carolyn when she first moved to California from Indiana. It was very easy for Carolyn, with the help of retired judge Len Turner and Carolyn's son Dick, to forge documents to take control of half of Fred's inheritance. Carolyn bartered sex for legal help with Love Judge Len to make it possible. Fred was bitter and angry after being divorced from Carolyn for 17 years, complaining often he was still working, schlepping real estate at the Lake, due to Carolyn's dishonesty. He, like Tim, was willing to help us against Carolyn. Anything to get even with "Mom."

It was amazing how much venom spewed out against Carolyn. I had interviewed 14 people and still had not heard one positive comment except she was good at her craft: separating elderly, wealthy widows and widowers from their assets.

Most of the fourteen witnesses said basically the same thing: "If you value your father's safety, do whatever is necessary to keep him from marrying Carolyn!"

We concocted a story to get Dad down to Pat's house at 10 a.m. Saturday morning. Bruce and I needed business advice or something.

I presented our case against Carolyn to Dad: she was a fraud, not the loving, family-oriented person who had come off the internet 2-1/2 months earlier. Her only goal was money but, more importantly, she was very dangerous and Dad's health was in serious jeopardy.

I tried to stay with the safety theme as opposed to money, which would be a much easier sell. The money approach could backfire with us three kids being charged with greed. Also, Dad could argue his money was tied up in trusts and a family partnership [which I wasn't aware of at that point].

His safety was the real issue anyway. I just didn't want to get side-tracked on strategy so Dad would think we were worried about getting his money. If we talked about money, Carolyn could also say the kids were greedy, that's all.

After presenting the evidence to Dad—-from all 14 people—-I braced myself for a fight. My assumption was we wouldn't be able to convince Dad that Carolyn was hazardous to his health.

Dad looked at us and said, "Well, let's go up and get her out of the house."

Unbelievable! A complete shock. Wow, that *WAS* easy! I guess if you present the evidence to a pragmatic, analytical person, anything's possible!

So the four of us drove back up to meet with Carolyn at Dad's house, several minutes from Pat's. Carolyn was in the back bedroom when we called her to come out to the living room. Even though it was almost 11 a.m., she was still in a bathrobe, looking pale and concerned.....knowing something was wrong. I began presenting the evidence against her, saying she had lied about the number of marriages, she had a criminal record, DUI's and 14 people "testified" against her.....and her true motives.

Carolyn feebly tried to explain away the extra marriage, but Bruce said, "Okay, Carolyn, get your stuff together and get out." Pat escorted Carolyn to the bedroom with "take my mother's bathrobe off!"

I wanted Carolyn to do more talking to see if we would learn anything else. I had prepared twenty questions for Carolyn, with hopes she would indict herself even more, like why she had—-according to Detective Howard—-seven names associated with her social security number.

Dad just sat without speaking, obviously uncomfortable his ex-fiancee was being humiliated by his children.

I had Pat supervise Carolyn's packing [Carolyn owned a gun!]. We let Carolyn know we would ship most of the stuff to her. She had already made several trips back from the Lake with her own things to put her stamp on Dad's house. There was a lot of her stuff already in Dad's house, which forced Pat to take out many of Real Mother's things.

While Carolyn was packing, I went through her purse, copying down her social security number, driver's license information, credit cards and bank information. For good measure, I took a couple blank checks.

I already hated Carolyn. She had taken advantage of our father and caused numerous problems. I had spent a lot of time on the phone building our case against her. It was fall in Chicago and there were better things to do than this.

I wasn't too happy with Dad, either. He had been very gullible by letting this Internet Whore convince him she was for real. He had a stroke four years previously, but Dad was still very sharp mentally, with only minor problems like sloppy hand-writing from the stroke.

I rationalized Dad's Internet whore mistake by his stroke, but I remembered Real Mom saying he was a sucker for someone blowing smoke up his rear end.

It took Carolyn forever to pack her clothes and belongings. Pat continued watching Carolyn while I carried her luggage to her car. I wasn't very gentle with her things, especially the big case of perfume and other cosmetic bottles, which were loose in a hard-sided case. I'd be surprised if any of the bottles made it back to the lake unbroken after vigorously shaking the cosmetic case and then throwing it into Carolyn's open trunk from ten feet away.

I peeled Carolyn's registration sticker off her license plate. Hopefully she'd get stopped for an expired license plate, only to discover Carolyn had been drinking. Last thing I needed was Carolyn slithering back to Point Loma while I was in Chicago.

Pat had a big garbage bag to put Carolyn's remaining things in. I made a remark about seeing if "you can fit the Lake Trash in there, too." Carolyn obviously didn't appreciate her ex-fiancee's son belittling his almost-Mom. She was not used to being challenged while engaging in "Elder Financial Abuse," a term I learned later.

We escorted Carolyn to her car but she wanted her disposable camera in the kitchen before leaving, said she had a few pictures on it. I retrieved the camera and had Pat and Bruce pose with me while I took an arm's-length picture of the 3 of us saying—-on the count of three—-"Fuck You!" while Carolyn watched.

Bye, Bitch!

Carolyn drove away with her camera. Pat went back to Dad's kitchen and ripped down Carolyn's Internet AOL In Love movie star pose on Dad's refrigerator door that originally attracted Dad, tossing it in the garbage pail. I retrieved the picture and stuck it in my wallet for some reason.

The whole Sting was surprisingly easy. I was glad to be rid of "Mom." Now we could get back to being a family.

Yeah, right!

Carolyn had married Tim for a lot less money than Dad had. She wasn't going away peacefully. She immediately had her daughter in Indiana call Dad, leaving a voice mail that Carolyn had cancelled a cruise with "Dutch" and broken an engagement to be with Dad. "Frank, you should be ashamed of yourself for treating Carolyn like that." Carolyn also had her close friend in Florida, Betty, call Dad, trying to refute the evidence. "Frank, you should be proud to have someone like Carolyn on your arm. She's a wonderful mother, grand-mother and friend."

Carolyn's son, who spent a weekend with Carolyn and Dad, emailed:

"Dear Frank, I can't begin to tell you the shock that I had when my mother told me about the course of events yesterday. I was in total disbelief. Had I not seen how happy the two of you were it may have been easier to believe. I did believe that in my conversation with your daughter she psychologically thinks that mother is replacing Pat and she feels threatened. At the restaurant her statement 'that whatever you throw away regardless of how small I want to see it first' led me to believe there was trouble brewing.

Fred Smith is hardly a fit character witness. When they first met he was quite dashing, but eventually the bottle took away his soul and mother supported him for years, finally choosing to end the relationship. He is very bitter and I worry about his stalking nature. He may not have told you that all of their friends as a couple are now mother's friends.

I don't think I have ever seen my mother so low and humiliated. She returned to her condo without electricity or phone.

I am certain my mother would be upset with me for sending this but I felt I had to get it off my chest.

Dick"

A few days later Carolyn emailed Dad:

"I cannot believe that you will not let me tell you about all the lies that Fred Smith told Pat. I can refute every one of them. I have the name of the lawyers and they will all tell you the same thing. The only thing I am guilty of is that I did not tell you about my brief, unhappy marriage to Tim Ruth. For that I am truly sorry. My heart is broken and I do not care if I live or die. The hurt is unbearable. Won't you even give me a chance to explain????

I love you beyond words and have never known the happiness that we had.

Please"

That Bitch!

I emailed Carolyn and copied her son [I knew Dad's password]:

"I don't care if you live or die. If you think we only talked to Fred and Tim you are sadly—-and stupidly—-mistaken. We have evidence from numerous sources, with the help of a private detective, that you are an unscrupulous, despicable human being who doesn't care who she destroys, so long as the money is there. It's also obvious your son was in on the scam.

You didn't really think—-with all the lies we heard from the beginning—-that we were going to let you and your son get away with it, did you? You may get away with it at the Lake, but not a nice neighborhood where we can easily spot a small-time fraud. We knew about you and your history in less than one week. It took one call by a friend living at the Lake. You really have a wonderful reputation where you live. ONE PHONE CALL to learn 'your father is engaged to the biggest Gold Digger in Southern California!'

If you think we're afraid of Judge Len Turner, bring him on. In case you haven't noticed, I love a good fight, especially with low-life's like you and your son.

You are two of the truly sorry people I've had the misfortune of coming across in my life, people who prey on seniors for their money after they lost a spouse and then destroy them.

We took the trash out that Saturday we booted your sorry ass out of Frank's house, the Lake Trash that is. As I said that day, 'Don't call us, we'll call you.'

Back to my original statement: I really don't care whether you live or die or, for that matter, your son either.

Bob Bradley ['One of the funniest men I've ever met']——Still Funny?"

Carolyn, as part of her phony campaign to win over the family, had copied me on an email to her son, raving about me and including the remark about being funny. It had been obvious Carolyn wanted to ingratiate herself to all family members.

In an effort to keep Carolyn off the roads so she couldn't drive down to see Dad, I reported her to the Sheriff's Department at the Lake as a habitual drunk driver, also asking if the .022 caliber pistol she kept "under her bed" was properly registered [Dad told her not to bring it to his house when she moved in]. I forwarded a copy to the Department of Motor Vehicles in Sacramento. I never did learn whether Carolyn's pistol was for protection or non-performance.

One week after we sent Carolyn packing, I emailed everyone involved, updating them that we had shipped Carolyn's possessions back to her and this "in all probability, would be the last communication regarding the lovely Carolyn." We had successfully gotten rid of her and now it was time to find a Carolyn-replacement because "Frank is lonely. Make sure they're legit."

However, Carolyn was calling Dad several times a day with questions about her things still at his house. Of course, she was using these opportunities to refute the "charges" against her, hoping to win Dad back. We tried to ship everything to her as fast as possible but she always found a pretense to call Dad about something.....a can of soup in his cabinet, whatever.

By now Carolyn was not happy with me. She realized I was the ring leader, spoiling her show. She had never been challenged by one of her victim's kids [I was 58!] before. She had gotten her town home, lots of money, trips to Europe and a good lifestyle by scamming the elderly. She was not about to let an amateur like me stand in her way. Besides Dad's money, she now had a burning desire to get even with me and Pat, the "Daughter from Hell."

Carolyn was good with emails. She graduated from newspaper personals to the Internet with her dazzling model-like pose in an evening dress, appearing in "AOL In Love." ." [Once Tim Ruth divorced her, Carolyn changed her name back to "Smith," her last name w/ husband #2, Fred Smith] Dad, when they first talked by phone, asked her if she still—-at 68—-looked like her AOL picture. Carolyn assured him she did but her hair was now frosted.

Carolyn, despite being exiled back to the Lake, was still emailing Dad on a regular basis.

At dinner at Pat's a week later, Dad asked me for a copy of the evidence against Carolyn and he began questioning specific pieces of evidence. Pat and I blew up. We knew he was asking because he was starting to soften his stance about Carolyn......he missed her and the attention he had been getting. Pat and I let him have it, saying he didn't care about the family because he was so selfish. He stomped out of Pat's house, saying "You can both go to hell!"

Carolyn bragged she could "refute anything." She had a lot of practice. "All the statements about me are from bitter ex-husbands" who didn't measure up to earning the right of being around someone of her caliper. The neighbors, ex-boss, others: as she said, she could refute anything.

Of course Dad wanted to believe Carolyn. He missed his sex toy and was lonely for her fawning all over him. At 85, it's not easy to find someone who could perform and service as well as Carolyn.

We were fighting sex with logic. See any problem?

That Bitch!

The situation deteriorated over the next few months. Pat became more frustrated Dad wouldn't forget Carolyn and move on. Pat and her friends tried to fix up Dad with some of the many widows at the Yacht Club, but it was obvious only Carolyn mattered to Dad. During this period Dad embarrassed Pat by explaining the "rules of engagement" to any new date he'd meet: no platonic relationships wanted! Carolyn raised the bar and Dad wanted to keep it up.

Dad and Pat's relationship worsened. He made it clear he was tired of all the badgering and wanted Pat "out of his life" if she didn't stop.

That would be a huge problem. We needed Pat to monitor the situation so Dad wouldn't become isolated, enabling Carolyn to weave her web undetected. Pat, who had lived only minutes from Dad for the last 16 years, felt betrayed since Dad selected Carolyn over his own daughter.

One time at lunch Pat threatened Dad with "if you decide on Carolyn, we won't be around because we detest her so much."

Dad: "I guess I won't be seeing much of you then." Dad was not someone you could easily bluff.

I cautioned Pat to stay on good terms with Dad, let me be the bad guy.

I was in San Diego a week or so before Christmas. I went up to Dad's house late one morning to take him to lunch, but he wasn't there. There were two phone numbers scribbled on a pad in the kitchen so I called the first phone number. It was the Harbor Island Sheraton—-ten minutes away—-and Dad had registered.

I drove to the Sheraton and used plants surrounding the bar area as camouflage to spy on Dad and Carolyn as they were having drinks. When Dad went to the rest room, I considered dumping a pitcher of ice water on Carolyn, but decided not to. Later I followed Dad's car as he drove her to nearby Lindberg airport, unloaded her suitcase and kissed her good-by, learning later Dad was getting serviced before Carolyn went back to Indiana for Christmas.

Lovely! Three months after booting her worthless ass out of Dad's house, it appeared all our efforts went for naught.

That Bitch!

I decided to try a new tact. Carolyn's last husband Tim said Carolyn wouldn't stay around if she knew there was no money. I started working with Dad's estate attorney Jack Ferris to see if we could tie up Dad's assets. Mom and Dad had several trusts and Jack had talked about a Family Limited Partnership [FLP] as a way to reduce estate taxes.

We spent a tremendous amount of time on the FLP and re-doing trusts. I continually reminded Jack the objective was protecting Dad's assets from Carolyn, not saving estate taxes. I told Jack to assume they would get married. Jack also recommended a prenuptial agreement if they married.

One of the strategies would be to tell Carolyn the money was tied up, she was wasting her time trying to marry Dad.

As I learned about trusts, FLP's and prenups, it became more apparent pieces of paper wouldn't stop Carolyn. Whatever paperwork we came up with was primarily for death or divorce. Carolyn had shown, with Geraldine and Fred, she could obtain assets from victims while they were alive, despite documents. Our paperwork might slow her down a bit, but it wouldn't stop her. With the help of Love Judge Len, Carolyn could illegally undo anything we had done legally.

For the next couple months Pat & I would take turns winning Dad back from Carolyn [Bruce, with 7 kids and 3 wives/ex-wives, had other priorities]. We would dig up more dirt on Carolyn, present it to Dad and temporarily win him over to our side. He would discuss the evidence with Carolyn, who promptly refuted or denied it. Dad wanted to believe Carolyn. She could provide more than we could. Dad didn't need Viagra to be around us.

Finally, after months of frustration, I decided to take Carolyn's last two husbands, Fred and Tim, up on their offer to meet with Dad in order to warn him what married life to Carolyn would be like.

We were all at Pat's the night before the scheduled meeting with Dad. We decided both Fred and Tim would discuss life with Carolyn before and after marriage, i.e. sex to no sex-misery. Fred would review how Carolyn and her son had cheated Fred out of half of his inheritance. Dad would hear it straight from two of Carolyn's victims: she was only interested in money, not love and marriage.

When we walked into Dad's house the next morning, Tim, seeing Dad's view of San Diego Harbor, said "Carolyn will never give up trying to get this house!" Tim also brought his new wife Susan, who had convinced him not to kill Carolyn. There would be a better life for Tim after he divorced Carolyn rather than kill her. Tim, indeed, had something to lose.

Both Tim and Fred realized Dad had been more successful so they started calling Dad the "Big Kahuna." The three men seemed to get along fine; Dad was gracious as always.

After initial pleasantries, I asked Tim to discuss life with Carolyn before and after marriage, hoping to show Dad a situation similar to his: Carolyn only married for money. I basically wanted Tim to say, in so many words, "Sex, marriage, no sex and misery."

Instead, Tim launched into a detailed discussion of how Carolyn had serviced him before they got married. I looked at Pat and Tim's new wife Susan, who were obviously uncomfortable. I could see

Pat thinking, "She's doing that to Dad!" Of course, I was thinking, "I gotta talk to my wife about these new tricks!"

I interrupted Tim and asked him to get to life with Carolyn after marriage.

After an hour or so of Tim and Fred's Carolyn-bashing, Dad invited everyone to the Yacht Club for lunch. I took a picture of Dad, Tim and Fred on the deck and entitled it the "3 Stooges," a comment Tim or Fred had made.

It was obvious Tim and Fred had made their point with Dad, who sent an email to Carolyn:

"To think I was ready to marry you. If you had been the woman you pretended to be we could have had one hell of a life together. It won't be easy getting over you but now I have to accept the fact it was all a scam. You and Dick were in it together, now the facts are clear. That must make you proud as a mother. I got off easy, so did Dutch. I don't know about Erv. I guess you are still working on him. You keep saying you didn't have a chance to explain, well now your two former husbands are willing to meet with you. Incidentally, neither of them is bitter. If you want me to arrange a meeting just let me know. If you get any good jokes keep sending them and I will do the same. I'm not bitter. We had a hell of a fling and I got off lucky.

Frank"

Pat and I had won Dad back and this time it was for good. No more Carolyn Smith.

Before returning to Chicago, Pat and I had Dad promise [in the San Diego Yacht Club parking lot after lunch] he would have no contact with Carolyn. I followed the meeting with an email:

"Dad, confirming our discussion yesterday, you gave us your word that you would have no contact of any kind with Carolyn Smith after we remind-

ed you that her record shows she is someone who prostitutes herself in order to manipulate seniors for her own financial gain. We have been warned by everyone that she is an evil, dangerous person who destroys her victims after obtaining their assets. We realize your health and safety would be in jeopardy if you continue a relationship with Carolyn Smith.

Per your request, I am forwarding two documents that were prepared while I was in San Diego: non-husband remarks about Carolyn and Carolyn's strategy to dupe Frank Bradley into marriage.

Dad, as I mentioned, we have all spent a considerable amount of time exposing Carolyn's true motives. During the past five months I have spent more time on this project than my regular job. You have no idea the emotional toll this has taken on Pat. People who you called to thank for helping expose Carolyn are now asking why is this nightmare still going on. It's time to move on with our lives in a positive direction.

Bruce, Pat & I would love to see you have a wonderful relationship [and even marriage] with a quality person. Carolyn Smith is no such individual. EVERYONE we have talked to says the same thing: she is a Gold Digger who destroys seniors who've recently lost a spouse in order to further Carolyn's financial gain. Her current victim is Erv, who she has been using as leverage to force you into marriage.

Dad, please remember Bruce, Pat & I love you very much and we only want the best for you. Your continued health and safety are our primary objectives. When we see someone like Carolyn, who would potentially harm you for any reason, it concerns us greatly. We are determined not to let that happen.

Love, Bob"

Two days later Dad sent an email to Carolyn:

"I worry about you. For the first time I called in the early morning and there was no answer and your cell phone was not turned on. I assume you are OK. Frank"

That Bitch!

As Tim said, "Carolyn will never give up trying to get your Dad's house." I guess if it's good enough for the President of the United States, the house is good enough for Carolyn Smith, The Commander-In-Chief of Gold Diggers.

On my next trip to San Diego I arranged for Dad to meet our Private Investigator Howard.

We figured if Dad heard it straight from the horse's mouth [Howard's], Dad would be more likely to believe all the dirt on Carolyn was true.

Dad seemed "sold" after Howard concurred Carolyn was nothing more than an Internet Gold Digger interested only in money.

Dad told Howard and me the retired Judge Len Turner was involved in the scam. This was the same judge who helped Carolyn get half of Fred's inheritance. Len showed up at Carolyn's town home at the Lake the first time Dad drove Carolyn back to pick up more of her things to bring back to Dad's house. Judge Len had appeared as the "trusted family friend," a retired judge, above reproach. Carolyn told Dad she had fallen hopelessly in love with him over-night and wanted to get a second opinion from someone she could trust, like Judge Len. Carolyn, of course, told Dad that Len had given Dad an unqualified stamp of approval and Carolyn, indeed, had found a real winner in Frank.

Carolyn's most recent husband Tim was impressed with Dad and decided to introduce him to Dixie, a very attractive 67 year old long-time friend. After Dad and Dixie met for lunch, Tim called to say Dad had outlined the "rules of engagement" about their potential courtship to Dixie: no platonic relationship; there had to be lots of touchy-feely activities. The bar was still up and Dad was determined to keep it up! So much for Dixie.

We suggested to Dad that he not outline the rules of engagement until the dessert course in future lunch or dinner "interviews" with prospective Mrs. Bradley's. At least let them get a couple glasses of wine in their system.

Bruce made a visit to San Diego. "Although the visit was nice enough, my lingering impression is very negative. Dad is a broken man. On our first day he said, 'I have lost my will to live and I am very angry that Bob and Pat blackmailed me.' He said he would live up to his promise [not to contact Carolyn], but he does not care about anything, sits around all day watching sports and mindless sitcoms, has started drinking by himself and is turning increasingly inward." Pat echoed that Dad was really down, depressed.

Dad's depressed state was actually good news for Pat. It meant Dad wasn't communicating—-or more importantly—-seeing Carolyn. Pat's disposition was inversely proportional to Dad's: when he was down, she was up.

Once again Dad bounced back quickly and it was obvious to Pat things were back to normal between Dad and the Internet Whore. One day Dad blew Pat off for lunch, so Pat decided to follow him when she saw his car go by. Dad drove to a restaurant in Old Town, obviously for lunch with Carolyn.

Pat was going nuts.

I wished Pat had gone into the Old Town Restaurant to confront Dad and Carolyn. It would have been great for Pat to whack Carolyn in front of Dad. Both Carolyn and Dad would get the message that Carolyn was REALLY unwelcome in the family. I couldn't hit Carolyn. A guy hitting a 69 year old woman wouldn't garner any sympathy, regardless of the reason. Pat could. Slapping the crap out of Carolyn [or dumping water on her] in front of Dad would have accomplished a lot of things.

Pat, after hearing my suggestion about future opportunities to slap the crap out of Carolyn, didn't seem to share my opinion. Pat probably felt more like slapping the crap out of Dad.

I sent an email to Bruce, Pat, lawyer-cousin Ronnie and Detective Howard soliciting ideas. Ronnie suggested Hospice grief support groups as a way for Dad to meet people. I reminded him that our efforts to involve Dad with any of the Yacht Club or other seniors were unsuccessful.

I wondered, should we meet with Erv to diffuse Carolyn's leverage over Dad? Probably not, because then she would be able to concentrate on Dad full-time. Plus, she'd really have a case for needing Dad's "financial security" if we chased Erv away. Carolyn had told Dad she needed marriage to insure "financial security."

Marsha Seff, Elder columnist at the S.D. Union Tribune, couldn't help. She could use our story, but without names and photos. Marsha suggested we involve Dad in nearby Senior Center activities. I investigated several Centers but quickly realized he would not be interested, much like we had seen with morning retiree coffee gatherings to solve worldly problems at the Yacht Club. Dad was not interested in platonic relationships until he solved the Mom-replacement problem.

Bruce, Pat and I continued to debate how much we should go after Carolyn. We were concerned that attacking Carolyn might back-fire, "chasing Dad into her arms." We decided to let it slide, see if there were other options.

In phone conversations with Bruce, Dad said "I cared for her and I think she cared for me; Carolyn never did anything to hurt me. We had a lot of fun and losing her was a real blow."

That Bitch!

Dad was starting to dig his heels in against us. Carolyn and her girlfriends, who were calling and emailing Dad, got Dad thinking about standing up to his kids. "They're just greedy. Why do you let your children control your life? They just want your money, not your happiness. Carolyn's the one who wants to make you happy."

Dad was losing patience with our interference. "It's my life and I'll do what I want. All Carolyn's friends tell me she's a wonderful mother, grandmother and person. So many people can't be wrong. You've been talking to the wrong people. Leave me alone and let me decide what's best for me. If you don't leave me alone, I want you out of my life."

Dad never threatened us with financial retaliation....about inheritance. It wouldn't have worked anyway. We were concerned about his safety.

The good news was Pat lived close to Dad, so it appeared Carolyn was reluctant to go to Dad's house since Pat stopped by Dad's several times a week. He also had a housekeeper every other week who did not like Carolyn. The housekeeper knew the situation and, if necessary, would alert us to any trespassing by Carolyn.

I was beside myself. Why couldn't Dad see what type of person Carolyn was? Why couldn't Dad see what this was doing to the family, especially Pat, who appeared to be on the verge of a nervous breakdown after almost a year of Carolyn? It was also taking a huge toll on me. I was spending so much time on this, flying to San Diego, I was worried about getting fired. With maybe 5 years to early retirement, I was not financially set to retire yet. I needed my full pension and more money in my 401k, especially with the stock market taking a big down-turn in 2001. I had never based my retirement on any assumptions of inheritance.

I couldn't stop thinking about it. It was driving me crazy. I was sleeping 3-4 hours a night, scheming how to stop Carolyn.

And projecting. I envisioned them getting married and Carolyn forcing him to sell the house. She would move out of the area so she could isolate Dad, obtain his assets and then kill him. Dad, too proud to admit he was wrong about Carolyn, would not call us for help despite horrific conditions Carolyn's ex-husbands and others warned us about. I imagined getting a phone call eight months after they married, saying Dad had died and his cremated ashes were being returned to Rosecrans National Cemetery on Point Loma. "Oh, by the way, there are no assets left." Click.

I had been warned by several people she was going to do exactly that...kill Dad....while I stood by and watched it happen. Then I would have to live with that knowledge for the rest of my life. Wonderful, just wonderful.

The game was over if Carolyn married Dad. She would control millions in cash, which would buy the best lawyers so we couldn't afford to go up against her. Dad was so ga-ga over Carolyn he would sign any thing she put in front of him. If not, she had proven she—-along with son Dick—-were not bashful about forging signatures. She only had to be semi-decent to Dad for 6-8 months, at which point she would have everything in her name, the expensive lawyers on her side and revenge against me for even thinking I could challenge Carolyn Smith. I could think about it for the next 20 years while Carolyn enjoyed the fruits of her labor.

The only option left for me would probably be one that would result in serious jail time. The thought of a low-life predator like Carolyn tricking a remarkable achiever and wonderful person like

Dad into marriage was completely repulsive to me. It was a situation I knew I couldn't accept, to think this scum would be responsible for the demise of someone who had been in the same league as Mel Laird, General John Vessey, retired Chairman of the Joint Chiefs, and other highly-successful members of Martin's Board.

I continued to research "Elder Financial Abuse." Books and articles contained similar recommendations: involve local authorities, lawyers; use trusts and a prenup. However, traditional options wouldn't thwart Carolyn. She was too smart—-and dishonest—-to let normal methods stop her. Plus, she had free legal help from Love Judge Len.

I asked everyone, even strangers, for advice. It was amazing what came back. Some said negotiate with Carolyn to buy her out. Others, including our private eye Howard, said to get Dad a nice, high-class San Diego hooker, or—-more diplomatically—-"escort." One dignified 74 year-old woman—-in the San Diego Yacht Club Jacuzzi with me—-suggested I have both Carolyn's knees broken. On a plane to San Diego from Chicago, a young doctor sitting next to me advised getting Carolyn to Ti Juana, where a lot of people "just disappear, if you know what I mean." Yikes! I guess the good doctor had his fingers crossed when he took the Hippocratic Oath.

My wife even bought a Voodoo Doll, which we stuck Carolyn's face on. The Voodoo Doll had a picture of Dad in one hand and small play dollars in the other. We stuck pins and cockatiel feathers, from our bird "Chicken," in Carolyn. We were willing to try anything!

My vote was a house call on Carolyn by Dr. Kevorkian. I'd even pay for his bail and plane ticket.

I talked to several lawyers about getting a restraining order against Carolyn. No luck. A 3d party couldn't do it. Dad would have to request the restraining order. Yeah, right!

Carolyn even offered to sign a prenuptial agreement, which gave Dad more ammunition Carolyn was "legitimate," not interested in money. Carolyn's victims reminded me prenups, like trusts, were for honest people. Carolyn was not about to be stopped by a piece of paper. Her track record, and town home, showed she wanted all the assets. She was not good at sharing with kids, at least not her own.

Carolyn voluntarily returned a $10,000 mutual fund Dad had bought in her name [probably to sweeten his marriage proposal]. She knew there was a lot more money than that, so why not return the $10,000 with "I'm not interested in getting married for money." This fueled Dad's contention she was a decent person, their relationship was not about money.

That Bitch!

I ignored everyone's suggestions about getting rid of "Mom." Carolyn knew how much Dad was worth. Why would she settle for a million or two buy-out [assuming we could even raise that much, which was extremely doubtful] when she could probably get everything? At worst, she would get all of his liquid assets—-millions in cash and securities—-and a life estate at the Point Loma house. At best, she would end up with all the assets including the house.....and revenge against Pat and me for having the audacity to challenge "The Biggest Gold Digger in Southern California."

Besides, if we offered Carolyn a buy-out, it would appear money was our motive. Carolyn had a history of lying and dishonesty; why would she even keep her word if she received a buy-out?

There was just one minor problem: all the lawyers I talked to, 9 or 10 of them in both California and Illinois, said we couldn't stop Carolyn—-or Dad—-from getting married. The facts she had a criminal record of elder assault, conned an elderly Alzheimer's victim out of her town house & assets and was a known dangerous Gold Digger to almost everyone at the Lake didn't matter. Dad was obviously mentally competent and Carolyn had done nothing to harm him or steal anything. I was getting very tired of hearing that statement.

I asked one lawyer, "You mean I have to stand by, knowing what will happen, and wait until she kills him?"

"Yes."

Lovely, just f'n lovely!

What a hopeless feeling. Dad wanted us "out of his life" if we didn't stop interfering, "trying to control his life." Carolyn would kill Dad and end up with his assets.....and I had permitted it to happen.

To top everything off, the law was on her side.

Dad knew he was special, the Alpha Male. He probably reasoned Carolyn dumped on her last two husbands because they deserved it. Carolyn hadn't been around a "real" man.....like Dad. No way would she treat Dad like she treated the last two Rummies.

Sex versus logic. *Ouch!*

I didn't know what to do, couldn't sleep. What a nightmare.... every day!

It was becoming apparent one of my options, if Carolyn was successful in getting Dad to the altar, would be to kill Carolyn. I didn't know how else to protect him from her. Pat and Bruce brushed off the "option," thinking I really wouldn't follow through with it. They brushed it aside, but I started thinking about ways to do it. Could I make it look like an accident?

Our strategy to introduce Dad to more women was back-firing. In a phone call Dad told Bruce that Carolyn was the "most fun" of all the women he met. Any allegations against her were "speculation" or we had talked to the "wrong people," not Carolyn's friends.

"I love Carolyn Smith and you three kids have ruined it for me."

Dad defended Carolyn, saying she was someone with high moral values. He said Carolyn told him "during her first marriage she was so shy that she changed into her nightgown in a closet for the first six months before getting into bed."

I told Pat, "that Bitch has screwed half the men in Southern California over the age of 70 to get their money and pretty soon she'll have Dad convinced she's a virgin."

Dad and we three kids went to Greensboro in October for Bruce's oldest son's wedding. The strain was obvious. Dad was "poor me-ing" it, hoping we'd feel sorry for him, let him have Carolyn. He said something about "we're just not a family anymore."

Pat was fed up with everything. She was almost to the point of hoping Carolyn would kill Dad. If Carolyn didn't, Pat might!

The only good news was Carolyn and Dad weren't married. No one was celebrating. Everyone was miserable.

The Internet Whore continued to whip-saw us, through Dad, around. It had been fourteen months since we kicked her out of Dad's house, nothing had worked. Dad was becoming more outspoken that Carolyn was his only answer.

Pat was drained after being on the front line, worn out from the back-and-forth with Dad. She railed on Bruce and me to stop wasting time "selling" Dad and go after Carolyn. We agreed but didn't know how.

Pat continually called me, often hysterical or in tears. "Why can't Dad see what he's doing to the family? He's letting this Internet

Stranger destroy our family. That worthless Bitch comes off 'AOL in Love' and in less than three months she's ruined family relationships that took a half-century to build. Dad can't have it both ways. If he is mentally competent according to the law, he's responsible for his actions. He says he's in his 'right mind,' then he has to know what he's doing and how this debacle is affecting everyone in the family."

Since Bruce had the best relationship with Dad, I asked Bruce to make an impassioned plea to Dad that the Carolyn Debacle was taking a huge toll on Pat. If Dad didn't want to see Pat have a nervous breakdown, he had to break off things with Carolyn.

It was becoming apparent Bruce's enthusiasm over this mess was waning. He said he would try to "sell" Dad that Pat was near a nervous breakdown, but it was impossible to know if Bruce would actually follow up on his promise. Bruce was reverting to his "jerk" personality, doing just the opposite of what people asked him to do.

Based on information from Fred, Bruce wanted to put flyers in all the Lake mail boxes to humiliate Carolyn, threatening to turn her in to the IRS for not reporting a minor amount of income. Besides the potential legal liability [or not being an effective strategy], there was the distribution problem to all the neighborhood mail boxes. Bruce had grand ideas on many things, but he had no intention of actually doing any of the work.

Lawyer-cousin Ronnie suggested we consider Dad was subjected to "undue influence" by Carolyn. We also thought about obtaining an involuntary conservatorship as a way to control Dad's assets so we could tell Carolyn to move on to her next victim since Dad's money was tied up. The problem with these options was Dad would have to be diagnosed as mentally incompetent by a mental health expert for a judge to issue a ruling. That was not the case and, if we tried, it would just convince Dad we were only interested in his money, not his safety.

Once again, a lot of wasted time but no solution.

Just when I thought things couldn't get any worse, I saw an email from Dad to Carolyn: "Since 8 p.m. I have been trying to reach you on both phones. Your one line is busy and the other you don't answer. I'll keep trying 'til I go to bed. I'll always love you. Frank"

Maybe it would be best to let them have each other, get on with my life.

Some friends even suggested I back off, let Dad have Carolyn. Why continue to humiliate Dad? He didn't have a much time left; let him enjoy the remaining years, even if Carolyn is a Gold Digger.

I had considered the option, however Dad was just too vulnerable and the evidence against Carolyn too compelling. I was unable to find even one person who had something nice to say about Carolyn, and Dad had lost his fast ball when it came to love. He was obviously having trouble "connecting the love dots," even though he was mentally competent in the legal sense. He wouldn't be able to defend himself against someone like Carolyn, and there was no indication Carolyn would treat Dad any differently than she had treated Tim, Fred, Dutch, Larry or her other victims. Why should she? Carolyn didn't want more love, she wanted more money.

Had I believed Carolyn would have treated Dad even semi-decently after marriage, I might have backed off.

No, Dad couldn't have her, at least not without a fight......a big fight. The down-side risk to both Dad and me was too great. I knew I wouldn't be able to stand by while Carolyn methodically destroyed him.

If Carolyn destroyed Dad, there was a good chance it would destroy me, too.

About this time I read a newspaper article indicating 50% of all passwords were a pet's or relative's name or the word "password." Getting up one night at my usual 3 a.m. time, I wondered if I could hack Carolyn's email AOL account by guessing her password in order to gain access to her emails. I had been unsuccessful in my attempts to access her emails illegally since it required physically installing a program on Carolyn's computer [according to a friend who was in Corporate I.T. Security; he sent me a program in case I wanted to break into Carolyn's townhouse, install the program on her computer].

I went through Carolyn's kids names [even though Carolyn was not a big fan of spouses, she liked her kids] and "password." No luck. I remembered, from the week of lunches and dinners during Dad's 85th Birthday week, Carolyn had a pet canary "Jose." I stuck in "jose" and then "jose1" in her AOL password and—-Bingo—-"jose1" was her password.

I was able to monitor her emails. I'd get up by 5 a.m. Chicagotime—-3 a.m. in San Diego—-and check Carolyn's emails. I was very careful, after opening an email, to return it to "unread" status when done.

It became obvious what Carolyn was doing. She would email her girlfriends with any allegations by Pat or me and then have her girlfriends respond to Dad by email or phone with a rebuttal. Dad didn't stand a chance. Carolyn had a team supporting her in addition to her sexual weapons. We had logic and talk about family values. Guess which one the big Vegas money was on?

Just before Christmas 2001, Dad sent an email to Betty, Carolyn's most influential co-conspirator, who lived in Florida:

"I know you recently talked with Carolyn and you know of our relationship. You are one of a few. None of her friends or family know. We have had to do a lot of sneaking around. Why don't you give her the same advice you gave me? Tell her to follow her heart just like you told me. You know her

thinking and her feelings and her choices probably better than I do. She confides in you and values your opinion and advice. So tell her. May you have a great holiday season. Frank"

From Betty to Carolyn, who copied Dad:

"Have email from Frank. He does seem sincere in his love for you. Hesitate to answer because I want to hear how you feel. Will send you his message. I just want you to have the very best life has to offer——you deserve it all."

Carolyn to Betty just after Christmas:

"Just sent my letter on to Frank as he wanted to know what I wrote. Would like for you to write him and say that you think I have this fear of him choosing his family over me again. Also, that it is a shame that we have to sneak around as I have never had the problem of anyone being ashamed of me before."

That Bitch! She was covering all the bases.

Carolyn to Betty, who copied Dad:

"Yes, I had a wonderful time in Canada [with Erv], however, I spent a lot of time wishing it had been Frank there instead of Erv. Then I really do feel guilty because Erv is so good to me. I have told you how dearly I love Frank. I can honestly say that I have never loved a man like this before and we love to be together. Frank is convinced that we can be happy together but I still worry about his family! It is so hard for me to forget the way I was treated but, believe me, I do try. Can't help wishing that you were here and we could settle all of my problems over a cup of coffee or hot chocolate. I'll write more later on——it is just good to unload and you always understand.

Scarlett [Carolyn sometimes signed her emails to Betty, other friends with 'Scarlett']"

It was obvious Dad had presented Carolyn with an open-ended marriage proposal.

Betty to Dad the next day:

"Dear Frank, you have not been ignored by me, just trying to come up with some help for you & have been talking with my dear friend Carolyn. I am still in awe to think your family will not accept her and be thrilled for you to have such a charming lady for a mate and companion. There is no doubt in my mind that she loves you very much but is haunted by the memories of her past treatment. It is very degrading to feel you must sneak to be with the person you love. Being in love is the time to be proud and want the world to see the treasured prize that has become your very own. My heart goes out to the two of you because you both must be [I know Carolyn is] fantastic people and need to share your lives. We are not children and the clock continues to tick. I hope you manage to come to a happy resolution. In the meantime I am here as your friend. Betty"

Dad's immediate email reply to Betty, who copied Carolyn:

"Thank you for caring. I know what a good friend you have been to Carolyn and how much you have meant to each other. I love Carolyn very much, more than I can adequately express in words. I would be proud to have her as mine. I intended to marry her and then my children became involved, but that is a long story. They love me but they were fed a lot of gossip and rumors, mostly by two of Carolyn's former husbands. In time they will come around. I have been a good father to them and they will see that only Carolyn makes me happy.

Then there is Erv. I have never met the man, but it is obvious that he is in love with Carolyn and she has made a commitment to him. That is why we sneak around. He does not want Carolyn to see other men so she can't tell her family or fiends about me or they would think she was two-timing Erv. He has promised to take care of Carolyn for life but I would too. As you say, the clock keeps ticking. I am older than Carolyn and the days fall to a precious few and I'd like to spend them all with Carolyn. Thanks again for caring. HAPPY NEW YEAR. Frank"

This was REALLY serious! Our actions against Carolyn had kept her from marrying Dad for a year and a half, but now she seemed emboldened, ready to make a move.

Bruce, Pat and I debated what to do. Bruce again wanted to do the flyers-in-neighborhood-mail-boxes to humiliate Carolyn, exposing her as a scam artist. Pat wasn't specific. She just wanted to go after Carolyn, end this debacle once and for all.

Carolyn emailed Betty on New Year's Day, 2002:

"Want to thank you for your help with Frank. I just want to slide for awhile. This is a huge decision. Let's make 2002 the best year yet. Love you, C."

Bruce changed his recommendation to a written campaign against Carolyn, threatening to have his ex-CIA friend reveal "factual information on you and your past to everyone in Southern California including your friends and family."

I reminded Bruce we would have already used any dirt we had on Carolyn. Obviously it had no affect. As cousin-lawyer Ronnie said, "You haven't scared her away yet."

My recommendation was the three of us personally deliver a letter to Carolyn at the Lake. Dad would not like it, but I felt we should demonstrate to Carolyn we had no intention of going away or changing our view. Only by delivering the letter in person could we get the point across to Carolyn. Obviously, we couldn't let her know I had access to her emails.

Bruce also wanted to make a big deal about telling Carolyn to choose Erv over Dad. To me it was irrelevant. Dad had more money [according to Fred] than Erv and Carolyn always followed the most money.

Whatever we did, we had to move right away. Carolyn said she wanted to wait "awhile," but I had no idea what that meant......a week, month, how long?

Bruce would not make a commitment about going to San Diego and started playing games since I wouldn't buy into his absurd letter-in-mail-boxes plan. I reminded Bruce empty threats to Carolyn would have no impact. We had learned nothing about her which would keep her from marrying Dad. Dad couldn't be convinced about anything, at least for longer than a few days, so why even bother.

We bickered for several days until Bruce emailed, *"We are in disagreement. You and Pat go ahead."*

Something had to be done. Pat was clearly at the end of her rope. I wasn't sure how much more of this fiasco she could endure. After "being there" for Mom and Dad during the 16 years they were retired in San Diego, the past 18 months of Carolyn Smith looked like they would send Pat over the edge. If for no other reason than convincing Pat we were finally doing something directly against Carolyn, I had to act. Or........watch Pat slide deeper into the Depression Abyss.

I wrote a rough draft of an email to Carolyn. The main thrust should be an implied threat to Carolyn about her safety if she married Dad.

This whole debacle was a business to Carolyn. She stood to make a huge return on her investment of only time. There was no risk. Some how risk would have to introduced, letting Carolyn know there was a serious down-side to winning the $10 million lottery. She couldn't continue to operate her business model with impunity.

On January 4, 2002, I emailed the following to Carolyn:

"It's been a year and a half since you came into our lives off the Internet. You were selling yourself on "AOL in Love" despite your story of having Dutch and many suitors who wanted to marry you right way. Realizing our father Frank was lonely after the loss of our mother six months previously, you bedded him down within the first few days and immediately began pressuring him into marrying you.

Everyone who met you that week of his 85th birthday party in August, 2000, smelled a rat. Your history and explanations just didn't make sense. We hired a private detective and quickly learned who you are: a dangerous con artist who preys on wealthy widowers who recently lost a spouse. Your last five victims [Erv, Frank, Tim, Gary, Larry] all fit that description. Since that time we've talked to 14 people, mostly individuals who did not know your ex-husbands, and every single person has said the same thing. We have yet to talk to anyone who has anything good to say about you. The only compliments we've heard were 'She's a good con artist' and 'She's a charming opportunist.' Because you are so despised at the Lake, it has been very easy for us to obtain information and assistance.

Frank heard the evidence against you in September, 2000 and agreed that you had to go. Within hours of leaving his house you launched a relentless campaign to convince Frank all the evidence against you was only from bitter ex-husbands and their friends. You've had your girlfriends and your adult children as part of a conspiracy to convince Frank that you are something other than a dangerous scam artist.

When Erv's wife died in 2001, you immediately went after him. Then you began using Erv as leverage to make Frank jealous, saying that even though you love Frank you have to stay with Erv because you need the financial security at your age. You've also used ploys like 'I won't date you, Frank, because it would break up your family.' You won't date him, of course, because you want to marry him; you want his money, not his companionship. During this time you have cheated on Erv, just as you cheated on all 3 of your ex-husbands while trying to convince Frank that you are a loyal person who will stick by Erv. As your record shows, though, you will only stick by someone until a better financial opportunity comes along. Throughout all of *this you've continued your incessant campaign to using your girlfriends and children in an effort to convince Frank that all the evidence against you is false. We, however, have not heard one single thing about you in a year and a half that changes our minds. You are still the same dangerous con artist who came off the Internet on Jun 29, 2000.*

Do you really think we will permit you to be around our father, who we love very much? Do you believe we would trust his safety and well-being to someone who caused the early demise of the woman whose town home you currently live in? Do you think we would permit him to be driven around by a convicted drunk driver who regularly drives under the influence? Or by someone, as we have been cautioned, who would kill an 86 year-old man within six months by altering his medicine or making him miserable? Someone who, after talking to 14 people, we still have not heard one good thing about?

This scam has gone on for 18 months and it's time to bring it to an end. We are not about to have someone like you—-with your record and reputation—-endanger the health and safety of someone we love very much. Marriage will not change our determination or resolve one bit.

We are telling you to end the campaign of trying to con our father into marriage. We will never accept you into our family and we will never accept you being around him, married or otherwise.

If we do, however, catch you in his presence, make sure you have the gun you keep under your bed with you. You'll need it!

Bruce, Pat & Bob Bradley"

Carolyn had to get the message: you can't spend $10 million if you're dead.

I didn't copy Dad because I knew he'd get my email right away from Carolyn. Even though Ronnie kept reminding us to stay on Dad's good side, I didn't know how to do it while still warning Carolyn to stay away. I felt it was more important to threaten Carolyn, at least have her wonder about her safety around Dad. This would counter Dad's "I've been a good father and the kids will eventually accept you" approach to Carolyn.

It wouldn't be a long wait. Dad emailed me and copied Carolyn:

"Bob, once again you have gone half-cocked. Carolyn has just called and she is turning your letter over to the sheriff. How dare you interfere in my life and threaten the woman I love. You guys are walking out on me. You must be out of your minds. I am in my right mind and able to make decisions for myself. I am determined to try to win her and no matter what you say I will continue. Only she makes me happy. I don't know how much time I have but I'd like to spend it with her if she'll have me. If you walk away from me it's your decision. I love all of you very much. Dad"

At least the family ground rules were established so we didn't have to pussy-foot around. No more worries about ruffling family feathers, "chasing Dad into Carolyn's arms." All cards were on the table.

I had no intention, however, of playing by Carolyn's rules, i.e., the law. Doing so meant defeat since laws were on her side.

It brought back memories of hand-to-hand combat training in the sawdust pit at Fort Benning. The Ranger School instructors taught us—-when it gets real nasty, down and dirty, one-to-one—-there are no laws or rules. Everything is fair: biting, eye-gouging, hitting below the belt. It only matters that you win, not how you win. Fighting fair didn't count if you were dead.

Anyway, the loser wouldn't be around to say Marquess of Queensberry Rules or the Geneva Convention weren't followed.

The old saying goes that anything's fair in love and war. This was both!

No way would I look up from Shelter Island to see Carolyn living in Dad's house.

The best defense is a good offense.

I realized I was the only one with enough balls or guts—-or stupidity—-to go after Carolyn. Others would be politically correct, stay within guidelines of the law. Not me! I would do whatever it took. All those witnesses couldn't be wrong. The vote was 14-0 against Carolyn. I was Judge and Jury; no question Carolyn was guilty.

Now it was important to see Carolyn in person to let her know I was serious about protecting Dad. She had to know this campaign would be more than just threatening emails. I would be in San Diego shortly for a two week vacation. Of course, there was no such thing. The Carolyn debacle made it impossible for me to relax or enjoy time off.....at any time.

That Bitch!

I would take a short trip up to the Lake to let Carolyn know, up close and personally, I wasn't going to stand by while she spun her black widow web around Dad. I wasn't worried about alienating Dad. I had already done that. If he turned against us that was still better than him ending up married to Carolyn. Then game would definitely be over....completely! There would be no relationship with Dad. According to Carolyn's exes, she would make sure by isolating Dad from us so it would be easier for her, with the help of son Dick and Love Judge Len, to get all Dad's assets on her side of the ledger.

Carolyn had to start thinking more seriously there were definite risk consequences to her pursuit of Dad.

Carolyn went to church in Rancho Santa Fe, the Beverly Hills of San Diego. She obviously drove twenty extra minutes to meet high rollers or take money out of the collection plate. Religion, like a happy marriage, wasn't a priority.

I would follow her to church and confront her in the parking lot, letting her know—-in so many words—-she better stay away from Dad.....or else!

It's not easy being on stake-out. One of the first things you learn is not to drink too much coffee. It was a very warm, beautiful Sunday morning at 8:30 a.m.while I was watching Carolyn's town house from a block away.....pissing into my McDonald's coffee cup and tossing it over the bushes. Stake-out learning point: look before drinking!

Carolyn came out just before 10 a.m. I followed her car, but she wasn't going to church. Recognizing me and realizing I was following her, she drove around the Lakes area. After a few minutes she drove into a long, dead-end street marked "no outlet." Knowing she would have to turn around to come back out, I backed into a driveway to wait. She pulled up to the drive way I was in, glaring at me with a "You're not going to win the Battle for Dad" look.

I thought about gunning my car to broadside her but decided there was no way I'd come out a winner, especially if there were witnesses.

Carolyn drove back to her town home. She pulled into her car port while I ran up to her car. Opening the car door, she leaned away from me while still in her car seat and screamed, "Don't hit me!"

I said, "I'm not going to hit you, I'm going to kill you if I catch you around Frank any more!"

Then I started yelling at the top of my lungs, "You cock-sucking Internet Whore, you stay away from my father or I'll kill you. You're nothing but a fucking gold digger. All you care about is money. Leave my father alone! I've killed better people than you in Vietnam so 'wasting' your sorry ass won't bother me one bit. I promise you won't be married to my father longer than one month before they cart your dead body out. I'll be happy to dance on your grave. Stay away from Frank or else!"

Hopefully my performance would humiliate her with the neighbors, convincing her to stay away from Dad. This had to be a performance Carolyn would NEVER want to experience again. It certainly was a performance I never wanted to experience again after just turning 60 [age, not I.Q......although close].

Carolyn, realizing I wasn't going to hit her, started screaming back, "I'll kill you first!"

After several minutes yelling we wanted to kill each other on a beautiful Sunday morning in a quiet retirement community, I ran back to my car to get the hell out of there before the cops showed up. Getting into the car, I looked down the street of town homes and, since many front doors and windows were open because it was unusually warm, everyone was coming out to see what the ruckus was all about. Many had walkers or canes and there were even a few wheel chairs. I cracked up. It looked like a scene from a bad movie. I stuck my head out of the sun roof and yelled to Carolyn, "You stay away from my father, you Internet Whore." Original, huh?

Then I took back roads returning to Pat's house since Carolyn would give a description of my car to the police.

Dad was not happy. He emailed me:

"Carolyn is not breaking apart our family, you are. You and Pat refuse to listen to reason. You are completely illogical. You will end up in jail. Carolyn called and told me you followed her, called her horrible names and threatened her. I advised her to go to the police. She did and they recorded what she told them and they advised her to keep her cell phone with her at all times and they will respond immediately. You are calling Carolyn at weird hours from

54

pay phones and she has recorded the times and the phone numbers and turned them over to the police. That is harassment. Let's straighten out some of the 'facts.' Carolyn didn't pursue me, I pursued her. I only received one call from Carolyn's daughter. She was upset with the way her mother had been treated. I did not receive any call from Dick or any of her friends. I surprised Carolyn when I met her at church. She had nothing to do with the arrangements. Erv is a fine, decent man, highly respected in the community. Carolyn has known him and his wife for 18 years and he knows her very well. Bob, you are going too far. You are eliminating any chance we have to reconcile. Dad."

Dad's church reference was when they met at the church in Rancho Santa Fe a month earlier. Unbelievably, one of my friends who lived in Rancho Santa Fe called me after he saw them. My friend had met Carolyn at Dad's 85th Birthday Party and knew her history as a gold digger [from me].

Dad in church! He was an agnostic and hadn't been in church in at least 10 years except for grandkid's weddings.

Dad didn't include Bruce in his email, just Pat, me and Carolyn. It was becoming more apparent Dad didn't think Bruce was against his relationship with Carolyn.

Carolyn emailed her two sisters:

"Always wanted to be 90 and have some jealous wife try to punch me out. Came close. Hahahahaha Anyway, you can see whose side Frank is on."

That Bitch!

It was just a typical activity to Carolyn. She was tearing the family apart. Not only didn't that bother Carolyn, it helped achieve one of her objectives of isolating Dad from his kids. Once isolated, he would be easy prey.

There was no turning back now. Dad had decided which side he was on. If we weren't successful against Carolyn, she would end up with everything, including his early demise.

Dad emailed me later that day:

"I have just spoken to Officer Jim South from the sheriff's office where Carolyn lives and he is preparing to lock you up. For your own good, please cease and desist. He has a string of charges: defamation of character, threatening physical harm, harassment, stealing computer files, etc, etc. You can contact him at 619XXXXXXX. Call him. I don't want to see you go to jail. Please stop. Dad"

I had learned a lot about Carolyn from her AOL emails.

There were some personal issues. Carolyn's granddaughter, April, was a stripper to "make money for college." Carolyn's son Dick, like Carolyn, was an alcoholic with a lot of skeletons in the closet. Any questions about the cast of characters were quickly answered by Tim or Fred. Nothing was more important to them than making sure Carolyn got her due.......after the years of misery she had caused them both.

Carolyn was also having minor surgery within a week to remove some "basil cells on her nose." I could only hope. It didn't matter what or who took her out of the play. Cancer would be as good as anything.

It became obvious who many of the people in Carolyn's address book were: siblings, grandkids, friends, relatives, co-conspirators to help win Dad over. All told, there must have been thirty people who corresponded regularly with Carolyn. I copied all the names, phone numbers and email addresses down long-hand because I knew Carolyn would eventually change her password or catch me.

It happened sooner than I hoped. I didn't realize you could tell on AOL when someone opened an email you had sent, even after it had been returned to "unopened" status. I saw an email from Carolyn's sister Ginny to Carolyn:

"WARNING! Sis, if you're not getting up in the middle of the night to open your emails, someone else is. You better change your password now!"

After three months, my days of screening Carolyn's emails were over. But I had the list of names from Carolyn's address book.....and I was going to use it!

My first email to Carolyn's email address book list was *"Portrait of an internet scam artist"* & included her evening gown pose from AOL In Love:

"This is Carolyn Smith's pose from mid-2000 when she was selling herself on AOL In Love, age 60-69, San Diego area. Despite her claims that 'Dutch' and other suitors wanted to marry her, she found time to advertise her charms on the Internet.

Carolyn Smith quickly conned my father Frank Bradley, 17 years her senior, into proposing marriage and, with 7 different names assigned to her one social security number, began moving her things into Frank's house. A private detective we hired and many people who live near Carolyn helped uncover Carolyn's unsavory past, identifying her as a dangerous Gold Digger who specializes in recently-widowed wealthy retirees.

Frank, based on the evidence he heard, agreed Carolyn Smith would have to move on to find her victims elsewhere. Before Carolyn returned to The Lake, she had Betty and Carolyn's daughter call Frank. Betty said Carolyn was a wonderful person and Fred Smith was behind all the lies Frank had heard. Carolyn's daughter said Frank should be ashamed of himself, that Carolyn is a wonderful mother and she had broken an engagement to be with Frank. That was the start of a relentless 16 month campaign by Carolyn and her cronies to convince Frank that the 14 people who told us Carolyn is a dangerous scam artist were not as credible as Carolyn's girlfriends and children, who said Carolyn is a wonderful mother and grandmother.

Amazing, isn't it, a woman like this has to resort to taking advantage of vulnerable men 17 years her senior? You would think that someone who is so proud of her own appearance would be able to find a companion closer to her own age. I guess lonely, 86 year-old men are just irresistible. Just ask Anna Nicole Smith.

Bob Bradley"

I didn't know what would work to keep Carolyn away. Maybe humiliating her to friends and family might do it. Keep trying, something might stick.

I also emailed everyone on her email address list other emails, including our Jan 4ᵗʰ threat to Carolyn, warning *"she better have her gun with her"* around Dad; *"You'll need it."* I indicated I had served two voluntary combat tours in Viet Nam and, if necessary, inferred I would not be bashful about adding to my body-count total.

It was important everyone knew Carolyn was at serious risk if she married Dad. Maybe a friend or relative would remind Carolyn to forget Dad, go after a "safer" victim. Being around Frank wasn't worth the cost of his deranged, dangerous son.

Once again Dad was not pleased. He emailed me:

"I am ashamed to you. You have hurt some fine people who have done nothing to you. You have disgraced me, your family, your mother. Did you learn that deep hatred at West Point, Viet Nam, where? I will not stoop to your level and say the things I feel now. You have hurt me deeply. Please stop and get out of my life. FXB."

I emailed Dad back:

"You've been out of our lives since you used incredibly poor judgment to go on AOL In Love to find your Internet Whore Carolyn Smith. You've been

out of my life since you sided with the Internet Whore against my sister who has been nothing but loving and loyal to you all these years. You betrayed her love and loyalty for your own selfish interests so you could pursue your Internet Whore's sex and lies at your family's expense, just like the other seven gullible victims Carolyn Smith conned before she bedded you down and started pressuring you into marriage.

You can stop threatening me. My mother taught me to stand up for what is right and I have no intention of backing down one bit. Carolyn Smith doesn't like it when people fight back.

As far as shame and disgrace, go look in the mirror and tell me what you see. I see a selfish man who has betrayed his family's loyalty for his own self-centered, selfish interests of sex and lies from his Internet Whore, Carolyn Smith. You did this even as you saw it was destroying your daughter. You said you are in your right mind. Act like it.

Carolyn Smith has duped you just like she did to Dutch, Erv, Tim, Larry, Gary and Fred. You're just a financial statement to her.

Shame and disgrace: As I said, go look in the mirror.

Last time: stop wasting your time with threats. If you want to pursue legal action, go ahead. I guarantee my lawyers will be better than any you and Carolyn can get.

Finally, I am comforted by the fact that my mother would be proud of what I'm doing to keep Internet Whore Carolyn Smith from joining our family.

Bob"

Maybe if I kept saying "Internet Whore Carolyn" enough, Dad would start to believe it.

I hoped my email to Dad would wake him up to the facts and remind him Pat was on the verge of a nervous breakdown.

I sent out a few more emails to Carolyn's complete address list.

Ginny, Carolyn's sister who had exposed my screening of Carolyn's emails, made it plain in a return email she wanted to talk:

"Would love to know more about this....details, etc. Yes, you are LUCKY [to learn about Carolyn]." [Ginny didn't know who had been hacking Carolyn's emails; Ginny only knew someone was opening Carolyn's emails during the middle of the night]

I called Ginny. She confirmed Carolyn was only interested in money. "If you can convince Carolyn that your father's money is locked up so she can't get it, she'll be gone so fast your father's head will be spinning."

There had been bad blood between the sisters. Carolyn was the looker, Ginny always a distant second to the attractive con artist who could land any man with "I've finally met the man I want to spend the rest of my life with."

Carolyn was the "Black Sheep of the family, always in trouble trying to land men for money." She had a history of stealing, even from relatives.

I asked Ginny why Carolyn often signed emails to her girlfriends and Ginny with "Scarlett" instead of "Carolyn."

"Oh, it's because Carolyn brags she is a modern-day 'Scarlett O'Hara,' a beautiful and vivacious schemer whose plotting can separate any man from his money."

Ginny also mentioned something Fred had previously said: Carolyn was probably responsible for the early demise of Geraldine, whose town home Carolyn currently lived in. Ginny said it was common knowledge Carolyn neglected Geraldine, who developed Alzheimer's, after Carolyn was awarded a conservatorship, keeping Geraldine in an unheated back room until she croaked. At one point Carolyn was removed as conservator due to neglect; somehow Carolyn obtained another conservatorship over Geraldine.

When Ginny visited Carolyn in California, Carolyn would take her girlfriends and Ginny to lunch. Carolyn always insisted on paying [with Geraldine's credit cards, which Carolyn tried to hide from the other ladies so it appeared Carolyn was paying with her own credit cards]. The person buying lunch—-Geraldine—-of course was not invited to lunch.

Geraldine's four brothers showed up for Geraldine's funeral, only to learn Carolyn had gotten everything. The brothers' lawyer said it was a waste of time to go after Carolyn or try to get back Geraldine's town house. A trial would be expensive, with little chance of favorable results.

I promised Ginny not to compromise her anonymity, and I was very grateful for all her help. To throw a little gasoline on the fire, I forwarded Ginny emails between Carolyn and Betty which bashed Ginny. Ginny now was more than happy to help me in my Carolyn Campaign.

She emailed:

"I am burnt up over the Betty/Carolyn letters. I am seeing red. All this time Betty professed to be such a good and loyal friend......I am heartsick....but glad I know. Just talked to my sister Sally [You would love her!] and she just can't get over all of this! Here is Sally's picture taken at work.

Please don't give up on your endeavors....I have a little plan......"

Anything to create turmoil, keep things whipped up, get help from Carolyn's relatives.

Ginny indicated my emails produced bickering within Carolyn's family. Carolyn was admonished by her grandson after a misunderstanding between the two. This was great news because the more turmoil I could create, the better chance Carolyn would decide to stay away from Dad.....in an effort to stop future emails from me. Just go away, Bitch, it doesn't matter why!

I asked Ginny for advice about stopping Carolyn. Although she wasn't hopeful, Ginny suggested letting the air out of Carolyn's car tires as a "warning." Ginny then said something I had heard before: get Carolyn to Mexico and have someone "take care of her."

Ginny was the third person to recommend killing Carolyn as an option. It was not only ex-husbands, now a close relative was suggesting it. It would be even harder to love "Mom."

Killing Carolyn as an option was becoming more of a concern to me. If she married Dad, I wasn't sure I'd be able to stand by while she destroyed him. It was repugnant to think a remarkably accomplished, decent man might be brought down by an evil Internet predator. That would be Dad's legacy.

From Shelter Island I'd be able to look up to see Dad's house, realizing Carolyn now owned the monument to a wonderful person's remarkable success.....after she had killed him. And I stood by to let it happen, despite being warned well-ahead of time.

That would be my legacy.

I had to stop the marriage or face serious trouble.

Carolyn's friend Betty sent me an email, copying in Carolyn and Dad:

"Mr. Whack-O, I have no idea who you are and why you name me as a partner in a scam of Mr. Frank Bradley. I have known, loved and respected

Carolyn Smith for more than 50 years. You have attacked the character of a fine woman and I want no more of your childish behavior. I have spoken to Frank for only a brief time and he seems quite capable of making his own decisions. Are you also attacking this respectable and kind gentleman? Be careful where you tread. I believe you are completely out of line and could be looking for trouble for yourself.

Betty"

I responded to all three:

"We don't like Trash like you and Carolyn trying to con decent people into marriages. Go on the Jerry Springer Show with the rest of the con artists, losers, cheats and misfits. At least you'll be able to provide some real entertainment value to someone.

Frank used to be a respectable and kind gentleman until your friend, Internet Whore Carolyn, brought him down to her level. At one time I had more respect and admiration for him than any other person I had ever met. I don't know the man any more.

Don't waste your time with threats. I've dealt with people shooting at me. At least they were honorable, decent people who believed in a cause, not like Carolyn, who only believes in money and how she can dupe people out of it. And don't tell me I don't know—-I have the evidence to prove it, which you will soon see.

Bob Bradley"

Dad responded to me: *"You bastard. How can you talk to a lady like Betty that way. I have to call in the police. FXB"*

I forwarded Dad's email to Carolyn's sister Ginny.

Ginny immediately responded to Dad:

*"AND YOU BASTARD....How can you talk to your son like that???
What the hell kind of father are you anyway? My Daddy used to say 'There's
no fool like an OLD FOOL....and he was right!!!"*

Surprisingly, Ginny responded directly to Dad, who would immediately forward her email to Carolyn and Betty. I promised Ginny
not to compromise her anonymity, but now Ginny had compromised
herself in one email to Dad.

Two days later Ginny emailed me:

*"My Son talked to Carolyn. He said to me 'Aunt Carolyn says you are
siding with Bob Bradley.'"*

Many on Carolyn's email address list were now aware Ginny
had compromised herself and she was probably assisting me.

Carolyn sent an email to everyone:

*"We all, of course, remember our attack of 9-11 but my attack came
last Sunday morning. I had received a hang-up call earlier and now know
that it was him [Bob Bradley] calling before he drove up. I got in my car
at 10:15a.m., not paying much attention to his car parked right around the
corner. I recognized him following me. He had a baseball cap pulled down
low and was driving his sister's car. He proceeded to follow me around the
area, then I made a mistake of coming back home. He then came up to my
car window and started screaming the awfulest profanities you have ever
heard. This was the first time I actually looked into the face of the devil. He
kept saying over and over I am going to kill you—-they will never find you.
He also threatened to get my son fired as he said he knew the president of the
company. My son's company now has an arrest out for him in Houston as well
as security around the company.*

*I am in contact with AOL since he has gotten all of your names. After
contacting his company, he was told to cease and desist using their carrier. His*

company has been more than cooperative and their many emails have gone over to the sheriff's office. He has since moved to Yahoo.

The deeper we delve into this low life the more we find out that he is one of the most despised people on the face of this earth.

Once again I can't say how very sorry that I am about this very evil, sick man disrupting your lives over the Internet. The Sheriff and several friends are urging me to move ahead on this and have him picked up. The charges, of course, would be stalking, harassment, threatening physical harm, defamation of character, hacking computer files, etc. Reading all of these lies has been very stressful for me and without the many phone calls and E messages of concern and support it would have really been difficult. I can't thank you all enough.

Bob Bradley does not believe in God. He is full of hate and bitterness and greed and it makes for a terrifying combination.

Please continue to remember me in your prayers. I will address a few more ridiculous issues later. Stay tuned. I love you all.

Carolyn"

"Stalking, harassment, threatening physical harm, hacking computer files".......like Bernie Madoff said, "Hey, no one's perfect."

"Defamation of character?" You can't be serious! Carolyn would have about the same chance of winning a court case as O.J.

I emailed Carolyn's email contacts, outlining her history of elder scams. My email continued:

"We have encouraged our father to meet many ladies and we have introduced him to at least fifteen. We would love to see him, at 86, get married to a wonderful woman. Carolyn Smith is no such person. After working with a private detective & talking to 14 people, it's obvious that Carolyn Smith is

a dangerous, violent predator who—-we've been warned—-would kill our father within six months of marrying him. Some have warned that Carolyn has already contributed to the demise of someone under her care, Geraldine.

Our father is mentally competent but, in reality, he's emotionally impaired and wants to believe someone like Carolyn Smith is sincere. We are determined someone with Carolyn's history of elder abuse will not be permitted to be around our father until someone proves to us Carolyn's reputation is not deserved.

We are also concerned about Carolyn's reputation as an alcoholic and her drunk-driving convictions. We do not want our father driving with her. I reported Carolyn to the State of California as a habitual drunk driver since she continues to drink and drive.

Carolyn mentioned the sheriff picking me up for numerous violations. She knows, since she has had an on-going sexual relationship with Retired Judge Len Turner [who is married], a crime has to have been committed before someone can be 'picked up.' Please don't waste my time with empty threats. If you have evidence, send the sheriff to get me. I want to eliminate crime as much as the next person.

Carolyn continues to use her neighbor Erv as a pawn to make our father jealous. Of course, Carolyn goes where the money is so she has no intention of marrying Erv.

Our Private Detective has uncovered humiliating facts about Carolyn, her relatives and her friends that could be very damaging. Our objective is not to hurt people. Our only objective is our father's continued safety and good health.

I do believe in God and I hope people pray for Carolyn. Carolyn Smith is the most despicable human being I've had the misfortune to meet. Until I met her, I had never met anyone who destroys people and families purely for money.

Until we hear differently, Carolyn Smith will not be permitted to part of Dad's life, married or otherwise. We love him too much to let someone like her in his presence. Our resolve is firm.

Bob Bradley"

Over the next two weeks I continued my Internet email battle with Carolyn's relatives, especially her son, daughter-in-law and Betty. There were numerous threats back and forth.

Several others from Carolyn's address book provided input:

>Carolyn is like her son, an unethical alcoholic with a "lying problem."

>Ginny is "insane and somewhat evil. She cannot be trusted."

>Betty is "a low-life, very rough, no lady."

I was also involving the San Diego District Attorney for Elder Abuse, Paul Greenwood, who was polite but not reassuring. I let him know I was preparing a packet about Carolyn's activities. He suggested obtaining letters from her victims. I was desperate. The law was on her side. I was willing to try anything.

I asked many of Carolyn's neighbors, victims and ex-husbands to write letters about Carolyn, which would be included in the packet to the San Diego District Attorney for Elder Abuse. Fred, Tim and two other brave people complied, but the rest refused. They were afraid of Carolyn.

Adult Protective Services was recommended by my lawyer-cousin Ronnie. As with many things we tried, it was useless. A woman from APS knocked on Dad's door but he refused to open it when the woman announced she was there to investigate an elder abuse complaint against Carolyn Smith. Besides, Dad would have to file a complaint himself. APS would not accept a 3d party complaint [from me].

I thought about asking Carolyn to take a lie detector test to verify her true motives. Yeah, right!

Pat called, hysterical. She was balling, railing on everything and everyone. "I don't care if Dad lives or dies. I'm so sick of this whole fucking mess I'd like to shoot him for what he's putting me through. If he's mentally competent, why can't he see Carolyn for what she is? Why don't we just let him have the Bitch. They deserve each other. So what if she kills him. At least I'll have my sanity."

At one point I took Dad's drivers license and military I.D. card, thinking he couldn't get married without proper identification. The incident was so upsetting to Dad, I had to "find them in his car" and return the cards.

Should I retire, move in with Dad? Even though I couldn't afford to retire, maybe it's the best solution. Like so many other "options" which kept me from sleeping, I put this one on the back burner.

I again called the San Diego newspaper, trying to get ideas from the author of a weekly column about seniors. I naively hoped she would print an article about Carolyn trying to con Dad. She didn't even have to ask newspaper lawyers about that!

I talked to several more people from Carolyn's address book. They echoed Ginny: Carolyn was only interested in money. She didn't want a man around the house, only his money. As with Ginny, I promised not to compromise their anonymity. Of course, it didn't matter in Ginny's case; she had already compromised herself.

Carolyn had been caught cheating on her first husband, which turned out to be a big scandal in their small Indiana town. Carolyn claimed she had been raped, so her son Dick decided to use a baseball bat to defend his mother's honor. Dick ended up losing some front teeth while gaining a felony conviction, which resulted in him not being able to enter law school.

Both Carolyn's daughters had experienced drug problems in addition to other issues. Yikes! This was sounding more like the Jerry Springer Show. One of Carolyn's email addressees commented: "Careful, you're dealing with some very slippery people."

I continued sending emails to Carolyn's friends & relatives with more information about the retired Judge Len Turner, who knew many of Carolyn's friends and family. I let them know Love Judge Len had been involved in the scam to get half of Fred's inheritance and was involved with the scam of Dad. In case they didn't know, I told everyone Len was married and had been having a relationship with Carolyn for over 15 years, bartering sex for legal advice to bilk her victims. More dirt confirmed by Tim, Fred and Ginny.

People cautioned me to tone-down my antics, I was out of control. Baloney! Being politically correct helped lose the war in Viet Nam. I had no intention of fighting this war against Carolyn with one hand tied behind my back, calling off the bombing like we did in North Viet Nam. If people didn't like my tactics or the resulting collateral damage, tough luck! I had done my homework. This war was worth winning and I would win it. We were 0 for 1 in Viet Nam. I had no intention of being 0 for 2 at the end of this war.

The retired Love Judge Len Turner wasn't finished with me! I had a score to settle with him, too. He had knowingly been involved in the scam of Dad as Carolyn's "trusted family friend" to put his stamp of approval on Dad. I was told he would continue his long relationship with Carolyn while helping her get all of Dad's assets. It was time to change his "un-indicted co-conspirator" status.

Obtaining Love Judge Len's phone number from information, I called one morning at 8 a.m. from a pay phone, figuring a 70-some year old would be up early. When he answered "Yes" to my "Judge Turner?" I knew I had the right guy. I said, "Is Carolyn Smith there?" Long silence, then "click." Now I would start screwing with the retired Judge, hoping to force him to plead with Carolyn to call off her campaign for Dad.

I called Judge Len three days in a row at the same time each morning from pay phones with "Is Carolyn Smith there?" It was amazing how fast he answered the phone, wanting to insure his wife didn't answer first.

Next day, however, I changed the question: "Are you still fucking Carolyn Smith?" He really didn't appreciate that. Next day: "Listen, you son of a bitch, if you don't call Carolyn off my father Frank, your wife is going to learn about your long-term sexual relationship with Carolyn and you've been part of several scams to help Carolyn get money. I have written proof."

Then I started calling Judge Len's wife in the afternoon: "Is Carolyn Smith there?"

"I don't know anyone by that name." Click. Love Judge Len would surely be asked about Carolyn Smith by his wife.

It was fun to black-mail a Low-Life Judge.

Dad didn't share my feelings. Carolyn had called him after she heard from the Love Judge.

At Dad's house, "Bob, your behavior is completely out of control. You are about to destroy a lot of people's lives. You know, don't you, that Judge Turner has five kids and has had heart problems?"

"I don't care if he has 50 kids and two pace makers. He has been part of this whole scam and I have no intention of stopping." This was taking a toll on Dad, too.

I was also calling Carolyn's pawn Erv regularly, asking to speak to Carolyn Smith. When Erv said she wasn't there, I'd tell Erv to ask Carolyn to return calls to Frank, Dutch, Larry, Gary or other victims Erv had probably not heard about. One time, not realizing Erv knew Judge Len Turner, I asked Erv to have Carolyn call Len Turner [Erv never realized all these people had the same voice: mine!].

Erv said, "Len, how the hell are you?" I was speechless. Finally I blurted out, "Great, Erv, how's your golf game?" After a few minutes of chatter, Erv agreed to have Carolyn call "me [Len Turner]." I was sure this would unnerve both Carolyn and Judge Len, who would be told of the incident by Carolyn.

Carolyn finally called for a truce. She would agree "not to communicate or have any contact whatsoever with Frank" if I would stop the emails and phone call harassment.

I won!

Tim and Fred were not as optimistic. "She's a liar; you can't believe anything she says. If there's money around, don't ever drop your guard. She will never give up trying to get Frank's house."

Sure enough, the nightmare would continue. Carolyn would not communicate with Dad, meaning she would not call him. Of course Dad was calling Carolyn all the time. We were getting his phone records from Detective Howard.

I confronted Carolyn about not living up to the truce and said I would start the email campaign again. She promised she would stop. Yeah, right!

That Bitch!

All this was getting to me. This debacle had been going on almost two years and I was worn out. I was just tired of fighting, couldn't sleep. I was mentally exhausted, worrying 24-7 about it. I had spent a fortune on trips to San Diego, neglecting everything except stopping Carolyn. The whole thing was consuming my life. Pat was on the verge of a nervous breakdown. Bruce, as usual, was no help. I didn't know how much longer I could keep fighting Carolyn…. and Dad. Maybe it would be better just to let them have each other. I was beginning to think Dad deserved the outcome I once feared. I was viewing him as the enemy. Maybe it's easier if Carolyn marries and kills him.

One night I was in Pat's kitchen around 1:30 a.m. working on my lap top when Ken, Pat's husband, came in.

He said, "I want you to stop the emails to Pat over the fight with Carolyn."

"I can't do that. They're part of the effort to keep Carolyn from marrying Frank."

Ken started yelling, "You son of a bitch, you're ruining my marriage. You're nothing but a worthless bastard."

I was shocked. Ken had always been a mild-mannered clinical psychologist around me. I thought we had a good relationship.

He continued, yelling "Fuck you! You're no longer welcome in my house."

I had never heard Ken curse before.

Now I was upset. "It's Pat's house, too, and I'll come here anytime I want. You knew my wonderful parents. Don't ever call me a 'son of a bitch' or 'bastard' again."

We continued yelling at each other until a groggy Pat came into the kitchen. After she realized what was going on, she told Ken to go back to bed. She obviously knew Ken had enough of the Carolyn Smith saga.

Pat said, "He's an only child, a spoiled brat used to having his own way. He has a terrible temper that you probably haven't seen before. He's blaming our current marital problems on this Carolyn thing."

The Carolyn "thing" was affecting all of us. Everyone felt like a victim while Carolyn held an entire family hostage. The fun factor had long ago gone out of this "Cluster Fuck," to quote Jon Stewart.

As I pieced events together, it became obvious my brother Bruce was instrumental in Ken's blow up at me. Bruce and Ken had lunch together the day before. Bruce apparently convinced Ken to take a stand against me. Knowing Ken, he wouldn't have done it unless there was support from another family member.

I made another call to my lawyer-cousin Ronnie in Florida. Out of more than 10 lawyers, Ronnie was the only one who held out any hope. He never, like all the other lawyers, said "You can't stop them." He had gone through a mildly-similar situation with his elderly father and his caregiver, so Ronnie knew our frustrations. All he said was "Don't ever give up!"

The more I learned about ineffective Elder Financial Abuse laws and Carolyn's "rap sheet," the more I worried about being forced to kill her in order to protect Dad if they married.

My MOS [Military Occupational Specialty] was 1542, Infantry. I was in the middle of my 1965 West Point Class academically. Post-graduation service, branch and location assignments were based on academic class standing. We only had five Army branch choices: Armor, Infantry, Signal Corps, Artillery, Engineers [all "combat arms"]. Additionally, 15% of the class [by thirds so we didn't lose all the "brains"] could select another Service besides the Army. The only

Branch assignment filled up when it came my turn to choose was Engineers, plus I could have elected to go Navy, Marines or Air Force. I selected Army Infantry, or "idiot sticks" according to my heckling classmates [Infantry insignia was crossed rifles, hence the "idiot sticks"]. The bottom 10 or 15 members of our class academically were involuntarily "ranked" into Infantry since it was the only Branch assignment left. Not everyone wanted to go to Nam as a "grunt."

"Signal Corps and four" was a common refrain from classmates not interested in making the military a career. Four years was our service commitment after West Point, Signal Corps was the least "combat arms" of our choices.

The mission of the Infantry is "to close with, destroy the enemy."

I felt if you were in the Military, you should be doing the #1 job: killing bad guys.

Hard to believe now, I was concerned the Vietnam War would be over before I had a chance to get there. After four years at West Point studying war and Parachute-Ranger training following graduation, it was unimaginable not being able to practice my craft. I had also been brain-washed into believing the "Communist Domino Theory" in South East Asia, which "justified" U.S. actions. Plus, I was single, so getting "zapped" wouldn't be as serious as leaving behind a wife and two kids.

Many of us were gung-ho: "Fuck Peace! War is our Super Bowl."

Although my first posting was a dream assignment to the Berlin Brigade in Germany, I immediately volunteered for a Vietnam Airborne slot. It was before the all-volunteer Army so volunteer Parachute Infantry Units were the Army's elite Brigades in Vietnam. I'd get $110 parachute incentive and $55 combat pay to supplement my $241 monthly salary as a platoon leader. Food and lodging—-C-Rations, sleeping on the ground—-were free. Life would be good. Only draw-back: thousands of complete strangers—-all named "Charlie"—- wanted to kill me.

After a year with the 101st Airborne Brigade, I voluntarily extended for a tour with the Green Berets as a Special Forces A-Team Commander.

More killing.

Carolyn's actions against Dad elicited thoughts of "closing with, destroying the enemy." She was clearly the enemy, threatening someone who meant so much to me. It was obvious Carolyn was capable of killing Dad, that she had already probably killed Geraldine. There were too many "dangerous, violent, ruthless, cold-blooded" comments associated with Carolyn to take this fight lightly.

Killing Carolyn didn't bother me. I knew I could do it, afraid I'd be forced to if they married.

But jail time certainly wasn't appealing. I had already spent four years confined at an all-male institution—-West Point. We used to joke that West Point was a "hundred thousand dollar education shoved up your ass a nickel at a time." In jail it wouldn't be nickels I was worried about. I didn't want to become some tattooed-freak's prison Bitch. Being married to an Italian from New Jersey was hazardous enough!

I wasn't naïve enough to think there wouldn't be jail time after killing Carolyn. There was almost no chance of making it look like an accident since I probably wouldn't have much "family time" access to Carolyn. According to ex-husbands, Carolyn would insure Dad was isolated from people who could protect him from Carolyn, like his kids.

She hated me as much as I hated her. No way I'd get invited to tea with Mom and Dad after all the humiliation I inflicted on Carolyn.

In court I could plead I had acted to protect Dad, who couldn't protect himself [my wife, knowing me better than anyone, would obviously suggest an "insanity plea"]. From my research ["I have this friend who's thinking about....."], it appeared 3-4 years in the Big House was the best possible—-and unlikely—-outcome. Dad would probably be dead of natural causes before I got out of jail. The good news, if that was possible: Carolyn wouldn't end up with everything after Dad's "untimely" passing, quick cremation.

I didn't discuss the possibility of killing Carolyn with anyone, even my wife. It if ultimately happened, last thing I needed were additional witnesses who could testify against me. There would already be plenty of existing evidence indicating my actions were premeditated.

This was not the first time I had been put in the unenviable position of executioner. During a radio conversation with my boss [our Company Commander] while I was a platoon leader in Vietnam, my boss directed me to kill a wounded enemy soldier my platoon had captured. Ignoring the order, I radioed instead for a medevac chopper. I assumed my actions would later be reflected in a poor performance evaluation report, but—-to me—-it was wrong to kill captured enemy soldiers.

Although I might be forced to execute Carolyn, it wasn't something I wanted to do.

Judge, jury.....yes.

Executioner.......no.

The marriage couldn't take place.

We limped along several more months. I assumed Dad was sneaking out to meet Carolyn for lunch or at a local hotel. Carolyn was in full hard-to-get mode, "hurt" from all the "undeserved" abuse I had heaped on her. Dad would have to earn his way back into her heart in order to once again win over Scarlett's affections.

That Bitch!

There was no indication Carolyn was coming to Dad's house, which Dad's housekeeper confirmed.

I kept reminding Pat to try to stay on good terms with Dad. She said she would try but she was clearly out of patience. Although I continually asked Pat to stop by Dad's house every few days to in-sure Carolyn wasn't there, Pat had clearly lost her enthusiasm, tired of playing second fiddle to Carolyn as the "scorned" woman in Dad's relationships.

We knew Carolyn was still communicating with Dad by phone since our Detective Howard provided copies of Dad's phone bills. I didn't know what to do about it. I had, after almost 2-1/2 years, run out of steam once again. I had to forget the Carolyn mess, pay atten-tion to my job, family.....my life.

"No Slack" was our Parachute Infantry Battalion's motto in Vietnam. The subordinate would salute the superior, followed by "No Slack, Sir."

"No Slack" meant we wouldn't cut the enemy or ourselves any slack. We could handle whatever Charlie, the weather, anti-war pro-testers or top brass might throw our way. We were in Vietnam for one reason: to close with, destroy the enemy. Regardless, the mission would be accomplished.

A week later I was back to my old self. Scarlett wasn't going to win this war. Ronnie was right: Don't ever give up. We've come this far, we can't back down now.

No Slack!

I continued my campaign against Carolyn's email list. Carolyn's son Dick reported me to the police and notified my company I had illegally stolen email information while using corporate resources [and company time] to wage a slanderous campaign against Dick and his mother. Dick accused me of "harassing phone calls, stalking, threatening physical harm, black mail, defamation of character & hacking computer files."

As Steve Martin used to say, "Well, **EXCUSE** me!"

My boss, on advice from our corporate legal department, explicitly warned me not to use my computer or any corporate resources. Dick threatened legal action against my company if I wasn't silenced. Dick also said my emails had hurt his wife's chance for a promotion.

My sentiment: Please stop! I'm getting all misty-eyed!

It didn't stop me. I switched to my wife's personal computer or Pat's when I was in San Diego. I targeted Dick since Dad had initially mentioned Dick was in on the scam [after Dick spent a weekend with Dad and Carolyn at Dad's house]. It was a stretch, but I accused Dick of influencing Dad to buy stock in Dick's company. Since Dick was an officer of the company and had also been part of the scam to influence Dad to marry Carolyn, as a new shareholder in Dick's company, I was "outraged" at the conduct of a corporate officer and intended to bring this sordid affair to the attention of Dick's C.E.O. As I said, it was a stretch.

My main objective was keeping things "whipped up" so Carolyn or Dad would eventually feel their affair wasn't worth the hassle I was putting everyone through. However, I couldn't forget Tim's warning: "She will never give up trying to get Frank's house."

Carolyn was also getting more reason to marry Dad: by obtaining all his assets she would have the ultimate revenge against me. Scarlett would be able to look down on me from Dad's house while I took a walk on Shelter Island.

Lovely!

Emails were flying all over. Some of Carolyn's relatives were threatening me while others on her address list actually expressed support for my campaign. One email I sent was entitled the "Three Stooges" and included a picture of Fred, Tim and Dad at the San Diego Yacht Club. I also listed all the victims—-almost 10—-who Carolyn conned, scammed or tried to. I always included her relationship with Judge Len because he had met a number of Carolyn's family members over the years and they had no idea Len was married......... or that Carolyn and Len had a long-time affair. I also made sure they were aware of Love Judge Len's sex-for-legal-assistance to help Carolyn scam her victims.

Almost nothing was off-limits although I decided to save some information—-like Carolyn's grand daughter, Lap-Dance April—-in case I needed it later.

I continued making 2 a.m. "raids" to Carolyn's town home, leaving reminders I knew where she lived, which would hopefully convince Carolyn she could never be safe from me. I made minor "alterations" to her car [missing windshield wiper blades, tacks under the tires] and, as things got more serious, considered putting sugar in her gas tank or spray-painting a huge "Gold Digger" on the passenger side of the car. Maybe she would drive around awhile before realizing she was a mobile bill board advertising her specialty.

I also investigated putting some type of LoJack tracking device in Carolyn's or Dad's car, but that didn't seem to be worth the effort since I was still in Chicago most of the time.

About this time I had a conversation with "Dutch." It had taken over two years but, thanks to Barbara from Carolyn's email list, Barbara had finally located Dutch's phone number and email address. Dutch originally met Carolyn on "AOL In Love" and planned to take a cruise with her. Although Carolyn met Dad shortly after she agreed to take the cruise with Dutch, she still sent her clothes to Dutch's summer home near Syracuse [he wintered in Ranch Bernardo near Carolyn]. She used this as an excuse to visit Dutch in New York to retrieve her clothes. She told Dad she also wanted to tell Dutch in-person she had found Dad, but Dutch, after hearing about Dad, said it was obvious Carolyn really wanted to visit his New York home to see if Dutch had more money than Dad.

When they had originally planned the cruise, Carolyn told Dutch that she "had finally met the man I want to spend the rest of my life with." Same act, different audience.

Barbara lived in Florida, close to Betty, and had gone to high school with Ginny. She knew Carolyn, too, and said Betty was just a low-life alcoholic who did favors for Carolyn to stay in her good graces. Barbara also confirmed Carolyn's reputation as a first class gold digger who was only interested in money. Barbara provided information about Carolyn's early years: men, money, mayhem. Who would have thunk it? Not the Carolyn I know and love!

Carolyn originally bragged to everyone she was getting married to a wonderful man so she would be moving to Point Loma with a beautiful view of San Diego harbor. Barbara found out the marriage was off, so she emailed Carolyn asking why. Carolyn's email response: "Frank lied about his age. He's 85, not 80." Sure! Carolyn was at Dad's 85th Birthday Party. Does she ever tell the truth?

Even though Carolyn changed her password, I could still monitor Dad's emails since I knew his password. He obviously did not realize I was doing so. It didn't last long. Bruce told Dad that Pat and
I were monitoring his emails. Why? I didn't know, but I was determined to get my pound of flesh from the Bruce-Meister eventually.

Despite the fact Dad changed his password, I quickly learned
his new password by watching over his shoulder while he thought I
was watching T.V.

Betty emailed Dad:

*"Carolyn has always told me she knew there was no future for the two
of you because of your family's total rejection of her. Frank, your family also
attacked not only me, but my daughter."*

I had sent blistering emails to both Betty and her daughter, who
decided to weigh in on Carolyn's behalf.

Dad warned me by email: *"Bob, I'll call Carolyn any time I want.
Stop your trouble-making. It won't have any affect. You'll just drive me to
Carolyn."*

Ginny emailed me: *"I could have told you a long time ago that you
didn't stand a chance against Carolyn."* However, it appeared my activities continued convincing Carolyn to "wait awhile" regarding her decision whether to stay with Erv or make a run at Dad. The problem
with "staying with Erv" was Erv would never marry her according to
Fred, who knew Erv fairly well from golf at the Lake. Dad had more
money than Erv so we had two strikes against us. Our third strike
was Dad had an open-ended marriage proposal to Carolyn.

Stopping Carolyn continued to be an obsession; I couldn't put
this putrid affair out of my mind. Sometimes I couldn't stand being
in Illinois, not knowing if Carolyn was with Dad at his house. One
weekend the not-knowing part became intolerable. I flew out to San

Diego on the spur of the moment without telling Pat. By this time I had worn out my welcome with Pat's husband, who was so sick of the entire episode that he didn't care if Carolyn married Frank. Ken just wanted it to stop devastating everyone's life, mainly Pat's.

After arriving in San Diego, I realized I shouldn't have come, plus I didn't have the guts to ask Pat if I could stay at her house. My relationship with Ken had really deteriorated. I checked into a hotel, hoping not to put any more pressure on Pat. She was clearly on the verge of a nervous breakdown. Last thing I wanted was more pressure on Pat if I got into it with Ken over something stupid.

I snuck up the steep hill to Dad's house around 9 p.m. to see if Carolyn was there or if Dad had gone out to meet her some place. The lights were on and Dad almost caught me when he came into the kitchen while I was lurking outside.

Nothing. Carolyn was not there. I felt like an idiot, especially after flying full-fare, staying in a San Diego hotel and returning to Chicago in less than 24 hours.

That Bitch!

People warned me about defaming Carolyn because she might drag me into court. That's exactly what I wanted! I knew Carolyn wanted nothing to do with the legal system....until she and the Love Judge used it to obtain Dad's assets.

I asked several lawyers to file suit against Carolyn over any-thing, nothing. Lawyers were reluctant to do something which might result in a "frivolous lawsuit." Wonderful! I couldn't get a restrain-ing order, couldn't prove "undue influence" or get a conservatorship, couldn't initiate a frivolous lawsuit, couldn't even get Carolyn to file charges against me. The law was on her side while she bartered better legal representation with sex than I could buy.

That Bitch!

It was obvious Carolyn was continuing communications with Dad for a reason: he was an investment and at some point Carolyn would want to see a return on her investment.

It wouldn't take long. Pat called to say Dad, at 87, had been diagnosed with colon cancer. He needed an operation right away, "in weeks, not months."

"Cancer surgery" for an 87 year-old potential victim would be music to Carolyn's ears.

Pat and I knew, after Dad told Carolyn about his up-coming surgery, she would attempt something. It was time for Scarlett to realize a return on her investment, cash in her chips. She had spent 2-1/2 years pretending to be in love with Dad; it was now pay-back time.

Pat was beside herself worrying about Dad's operation in two weeks, which might trigger action by Carolyn. I tried to reassure Pat with "I'm only 4 hours from San Diego." We were both petrified.

Prior to learning about Dad's up-coming surgery, Pat had planned a big party which would be a week before Dad's operation. Dad would not attend, but he kept asking Pat about the party. Shaken, Pat called to say she was getting more suspicious Carolyn and Dad had something planned while Pat was tied up at her house party. I reminded Pat, "I'm 4 hours away!" I booked a flight to San Diego just in case.

Pat called me at work the morning of the party. It was obvious she was extremely upset, absolutely positive something was going to happen that night. I drove home, packed in 10 minutes and raced to O'Hare. 4 hours later I landed in San Diego.

Without telling Dad I was in San Diego, I attended Pat's party with plans to go up to Dad's early the following morning. I assumed Dad would meet Carolyn at a local hotel to get serviced before he went in for his operation the following week.

I woke up at Pat's house at 4 a.m, 6 a.m. Chicago time, drove to Dad's house. For some reason his car was in the carport, not his garage where it usually was. That's because Carolyn's car was in his garage. I immediately went back to Pat's, woke her and we both returned to Dad's around 4:40 a.m. Just in case, I wanted another witness on my side.

Pat had a key; we went to Dad's bedroom where Carolyn and Dad were sleeping.

I turned on the light, telling Carolyn, "Get dressed and get out of here. We know you're just after money."

"You chased me away two years ago, but this time I'm not leaving!"

I repeated my statement. Carolyn said she was not leaving. Dad, who had taken Carolyn to Fiddler's Green Restaurant the night before and had a lot to drink, seemed groggy and out of it.

I didn't know what to do. For some reason I decided to grab the covers and pull them off the bed. Carolyn and Dad were nude..... and Pat obviously didn't think pulling the covers off was such a good idea. I only wished I had brought a camera so I could plaster Carolyn's sorry nude ass all over the Internet.

Carolyn, whose sorry ass actually looked pretty damned good in the nude at age 71, scrambled out of bed into the bathroom to get dressed. She came out quickly, admonishing Dad to get dressed. It was surprising how she ordered him around like he was a 5 year old kid.

What now? I couldn't force her to leave. Dad obviously wanted her there.

I decided to call 911 to report someone was trespassing on Dad's property. Before hanging up, the dispatcher asked if there were any guns in the house. I was about to say "No" because Dad didn't have any, but I remembered Dad said Carolyn asked if she should bring her gun with her when she first moved into the house 2-1/2 years earlier. He told her "No," so I told the dispatcher, "I don't know if there are any guns in the house," not sure whether Carolyn brought her gun along this time.

Twenty minutes later there was a loud knock at the door followed by "San Diego Police." I opened the door to see 5 members of the Swat Team, dressed in black and fully-armed with M-16 rifles..... and a German Shepard police dog. This was for two people whose total age was 158!

The Police Sergeant separated the 4 of us into different rooms and began questioning. Fifteen minutes later he came back to me: "We have a problem. Your father is mentally competent and Carolyn has not hurt him or stolen anything. Your father wants Carolyn to stay and you & your sister to leave. If you refuse to leave, I'll have to arrest you."

"I'm not leaving. You can arrest me, but I'm not going. Carolyn is a dangerous Internet Whore so I'm staying." Carolyn obviously didn't appreciate my official description of her to the Police Sergeant.

The Sergeant went back to Dad, who changed his mind and agreed to let me stay. As much as Dad detested my actions against Carolyn, as a father he didn't want his son going to jail........................
..........I think.

Five minutes later the Sergeant got all 4 of us together, announcing he was leaving and I was not to touch Carolyn. If I did, the police would come back and arrest me.

I told the Sergeant I had a copy of the report about Carolyn I had provided to the District Attorney for Elder Abuse, and I wanted my D.A. Report included in his police report. I mentioned my report contained damaging information from Carolyn's relatives. The Sergeant wasn't particularly happy, but he finally agreed to take a copy and include it in his police report.

My packet to the D.A. included emails by Ginny, several letters from Tim, Fred and others about Carolyn's history of scamming elders in addition to her true motives with Dad.

Carolyn watched with interest as I retrieved a copy from the car and made a big deal about giving it to the Sergeant, repeating that the San Diego District Attorney for Elder Abuse Paul Greenwood also had one.

The police had spent enough time on two people totaling 158 years of age. The Sergeant reminded me again not to harm Carolyn "or else."

The Swat Team left, leaving Pat, Dad, Carolyn and me standing in Dad's foyer at 6 a.m. looking at each other.

What now? All 4 of us go to breakfast for an Ihop Special?

I said, "Carolyn, get out. You're an Internet Whore. You only want money." She refused, repeating "You chased me away two years ago but this time I'm not leaving."

I looked at Carolyn, saying "You have 10 minutes to get out. If you don't leave, the phone calls will start. The first call will be to Erv, letting him know you've used him as a pawn over the past 2-1/2 years to make Frank jealous. I have your emails to Betty to prove it. The second phone call will be to Judge Turner's wife, exposing your 15-year sexual relationship with her husband, and the judge was a co-conspirator to dupe Frank out of his money. The last phone calls will be to your relatives....about your granddaughter April's activities as a stripper."

"But!"

"You have 9-1/2 minutes to get out."

Five minutes later Dad came over to me and said Carolyn was leaving. I was very surprised but relieved.

Dad escorted Carolyn out to her car. He opened the car door for her and they kissed. I walked over to Carolyn and Dad standing by her car.

"Carolyn, if I ever catch you around my father again, I'll kill you! This is your final warning." Both Carolyn and Dad had to believe I was completely irrational, actually capable of killing Carolyn.

Carolyn: "I've been taking target practice, so I'll kill you first."

Carolyn drove away. Dad went into his house without saying a word. He locked the door while Pat and I stood outside.

Pat and I returned to her house. I sent an email to Carolyn's two sisters and brother, asking them to implore their sister Carolyn to leave my 87 year old father alone. I related the incident which just took place and noted that Carolyn was trying to take advantage of an elderly man who was about to undergo cancer surgery. Also in my email to Carolyn's siblings:

>We provided a packet of evidence to the DA for Elder Abuse, Paul Greenwood, that Betty and Len Turner were involved in the scam. Also included in the packet were letters about Carolyn's efforts

to scam the retired banker and Carolyn had probably contributed to the demise of Geraldine.

>I had obtained embarrassing and humiliating personal information about Carolyn's relatives but my "objective was not to hurt anyone." My only goal was to protect the health and safety of Frank Bradley.

I closed the email with:

"The purpose of this email is to reiterate Carolyn Smith will NEVER be permitted to be around Frank Bradley, married or otherwise. Frank Bradley's children have been warned by numerous people that Carolyn Smith poses a real and immediate danger to Frank Bradley's health and safety. I ask you, as decent siblings of Carolyn Smith—-who obviously understand the Bradley children's concern for a wonderful parent—-to impress upon Carolyn our outrage at her brazen exploitation of an 87 year-old, vulnerable man: Frank Bradley. This nightmare has gone on long enough and it's time to bring it to a close. With Dad's up-coming cancer surgery, we need to concentrate all our efforts on his health without having to worry about Carolyn Smith's strategy to scam him out of his assets.

Thank you for your consideration in this matter.

Bob Bradley

PS I will be happy to send you the packet we provided to the District Attorney for Elder Abuse in addition to my phone number if you wish further information"

Since I knew one of Carolyn's siblings would send copies of the email to both Carolyn and Dick, I emphasized involving the District Attorney for Elder Abuse and the fact we had provided evidence to him. Carolyn had seen me make a big deal about giving the DA Packet to the Swat Team Sergeant, and Carolyn also knew her sister Ginny had sided with us. Would it finally be enough to keep Carolyn away?

Dad wouldn't let me in his house the next day, saying "Leave me alone, go away."

He was upset, for good reason. I had humiliated him in front of Carolyn and called the police into his home.

Dad dead-bolted locks from inside so I took several doors off their hinges and finally confronted Dad in the second bedroom where he typically watched T.V. Dad looked like a broken man. He said he wouldn't have the colon cancer surgery in a week.

I talked to him like I was the father and he was the son. "Dad, you've been very selfish about this entire affair. You're mentally competent, able to piece the evidence together that Carolyn Smith is only interested in your money. You've let her come in and tear apart our family and you've picked a complete stranger over your own children. This whole mess has almost destroyed your daughter."

I continued, "Dad, it's time to get back as a family. We love you very much. I want you to promise me you're going to have surgery next week." He didn't answer but I was sure he would have the surgery.

Dad did have the surgery, got a clean bill of health from his surgeon. He was still amazing. At 87, he was released from the hospital after major surgery in only three days.

I sent a blistering email to Carolyn, stating she had gone back on her "promise and word to have no contact with Frank Bradley." I threatened to ramp up my actions if she did not agree to comply with our original agreement.

"The facts and the evidence are ample proof, as the San Diego District Attorney's office now realizes. If you don't believe me, call them. Paul Greenwood [DA] was out of the office on Friday and I'm not sure he's back tomor-

row, but you can talk to Larry Buckeye, who's an attorney in Paul's office. You can also talk to Greg Brown in the Public Guardian's Office.

MY TERMS WILL BE MET OR I WILL PROCEED WITH MY PLAN. I STRONGLY URGE YOU, FOR YOUR OWN GOOD, TO COMPLY WITH MY TERMS. I WILL ACCEPT NOTHING LESS."

Carolyn responded:

"I will not send you anything in writing. I do not trust you or your sister any further than I could throw you. You are deceitful and conniving. I will, however, send it to Bruce and he can forward it.

Frank persuaded me to see him despite the agreement but he will not in the future. I guarantee it. He has proposed many times but he knows that I want NO connection with you whatever.

Your slanderous remarks about Geraldine do not even merit a reply. I have 21 letters about my good care from doctors and beauty operators. I have never harmed or duped anyone in my entire life. The Adult Protective Agency is pressing me to have you arrested at your place of business and assures me that this time it will be a felony. They take stalking and harassment quite seriously, especially of a senior citizen. It seems that many know about your uncontrollable temper.

Betty is a dear and treasured friend who dates back to grade school. She is guilty of nothing.

When my attorney called Paul Greenwood's office [she's a friend of his], she was told by the secretary that there was no file named 'Bradley.' Strange! Don't worry, I intend to talk with them all.

Sure, you don't want to hurt anyone. Mr. Turner has had a triple bypass and Erv is battling prostate cancer. And last but not least is your father who is going through a critical time.

I truly feel sorry for the greed that consumes you. I have told you that I am willing to sign that I will NEVER have any contact, in any way, with Frank ever again. I will not acknowledge or admit to anything else as it would not be true. You do what you have to do. May God have mercy on your soul.

I am hoping that this can all be avoided once and for all but if not I am ready. I shall be happy to email Bruce right away."

A few days later I received the following email from Ginny:

"Dear Aunt Ginny,

I can't understand the hatred in one's heart to be hurtful to one's sister. How could you support Bob Bradley to hurt mother? This man is deranged and now has threatened to kill her before witnesses. You have certainly fueled the fires. I will pray for you as you are deeply disturbed not to stand up for your own sister. My mother has always been there for you when you needed help. It is unfortunate that your own emails are being subpoenaed in his criminal charges in San Diego.

God bless you, and forgive you.

Dick

p.s. Tell your daughter that I am also disappointed"

Ginny sent me Dick's email to her, saying he would block any future emails from Aunt Ginny. Carolyn and Dick were some tag-team match!

I had surmised both Carolyn and son Dick were concerned about my submissions to District Attorney Paul Greenwood and the police department. I was beginning to think my prediction Carolyn wanted nothing to do with the legal system might be correct, especially since she and Dick realized Ginny had been siding with me.

After she sent me the email saying there was nothing in the District Attorney files about "Bradley," I not-so-politely informed her it was because the DA's file was "listed under 'Carolyn Smith.' Frank Bradley is the victim of your abuse. The file is under the Predator— -YOU, not the victim." Apparently she confirmed "Carolyn Smith" was in the DA Files because I heard nothing more about it from Carolyn.

Betty emailed Dad:

"Dear Frank,

Your recent medical condition causes me to have a heavy heart and wish you only the best. It is a very sad state of affairs that you must face this terrible news and have to face such a health problem without someone who loves you at your side. I truly applaud your zest for life *and the fact you must be such a vital, interesting and attractive man to still be able to seduce the lovely Carolyn Smith.*

Carolyn and I have never been in a conspiracy to entrap you or otherwise dupe you from your children's inheritance and all that rightfully belongs to them. What was wrong with a little happiness for you at this time of your life with Carolyn, who found you so overwhelmingly charming?

It is just beyond my comprehension why this has happened and why your children have attacked Carolyn and found it necessary to send their vitriolic messages to all her siblings, her friends and even my children.

Frank, I know you and Carolyn have found a few hours of fun and frivolity. I only wish you had been allowed more of those hours. We have only spoken on the phone and it is my loss to never been allowed to know you better. You and I certainly know there was never any conspiracy on the part of my friend and me. What a LIE.

My love and best wishes to you—-you are a great man.

Love,

Betty"

I emailed her back:

"Trailer Trash Betty,

Let's not get maudlin over this. It doesn't take vitality, attractiveness and being interesting to seduce the lovely Carolyn Smith. She's an Internet Whore so it only takes a good financial statement and Trash like you to gang up an 87 year-old man who's had a stroke.

Your email confirms what I've said all along: you are a low-life scum bag who has been part of the conspiracy to dupe Frank Bradley over the past two years.

Bob Bradley"

Of course, I copied Carolyn's email address list as usual. Carolyn needed reminding all emails to Dad had to stop, even those from Betty.

When in doubt, keep things whipped up.

I didn't know how aggressive Carolyn would continue to be, but if I could just get through 2003 I might be "home-free" since I planned to retire in early 2004. Once again I considered retiring early, right then. I decided to continue my campaign against Carolyn, see how things transpired. I really couldn't afford to retire since the stock market still had not yet bounced back and I needed my full pension.

During 2003 I spent a lot of time in Phoenix on business, which enabled me to drop-in unannounced often to San Diego, hopefully keeping Dad wondering about my whereabouts. Pat checked with Dad's housekeeper to insure Carolyn wasn't visiting.

I finally retired in April, 2004. What a relief! Now I could be near Dad 24-7 so there would be much less chance Carolyn might make a move on Dad.

Being retired in San Diego would hopefully give me a chance to repair my relationship with Dad. He was still one of the remarkable people I had been around in my life and I loved him very much. Although Pat was not as forgiving, I tried to put the Carolyn mess in the past but I knew the nightmare would not "officially" be over until either Dad or Carolyn was dead.

Carolyn's son Dick was actually my biggest concern. According to Tim and Fred, Dick had an alcohol problem and a tendency to switch jobs frequently. Last thing I needed was son Dick out of a job, forcing "Mom" to run Dad over to Mexico for a quick marriage in order to keep son Dick from going down the tubes financially.

After retiring to San Diego, I saw Dad twice a day, once in the morning and once at night, for the next three years.

I'd take him out to dinner or bring something to him. He was still a Horn Dog. He preferred another Yacht Club over his own Club because, at 90, he thought he had a better chance to pick up women. The Silver Fox was still on the prowl! Ouch! I was getting concerned we wouldn't be able to close his coffin lid due to all the Viagra in his system.

Dad continued searching the Internet for someone like Carolyn, with predictably disastrous results. One Internet Queen showed up on Thanksgiving Day for a long weekend with Dad. During Thanksgiving dinner she babbled non-stop about nothing to the dismay of the other 7 Thanksgiving dinner guests. Pat and I retreated to the kitchen at one point. Pat started laughing uncontrollably while I said, "Nice date, Dad," picking up a huge kitchen knife and pretending to commit hara-kiri.

Dad's Thanksgiving Internet Queen was gone before the sun could set on her.

I tried to bring back humor. I "reported" to Dad every morning at 0700 hours, sometimes wearing a plastic Nazi helmet, gave him a snappy salute followed by "Colonel, we have a problem. Your Eastern Flank has collapsed, your Western Flank is in retreat and you need a _____ [shave, haircut, shower, whatever was appropriate]. What do you want to do?"

He usually replied with "Damned if I know. Tell my troops to attack!"

Dad still had a quick mind which produced great quips. One time we took him to a new medical specialist. After examining Dad, the Doctor asked, "Mister Bradley, how old are you?"

Dad: "Ninety."

Doctor: "Wow! You look great for ninety."

Dad: "You should have seen me at eighty-nine!"

It took a while, but our relationship slowly improved. Dad stopped driving at age 90 and I had to help him shave and shower during his last year or so. I wanted him to know I still revered and loved him very much.

My rage gradually began to subside. Fighting Carolyn, son Dick, Dad, Bruce, the Love Judge, the legal system and Betty for so long had left its mark. I was continually angry, lashing out for no apparent reason. Plus, I was always tired, unable to sleep more than 3-4 hours at a time, wondering what Carolyn would pull next. It had been combat all over again.

Dad became jaundiced at age 91-1/2 while still living at home. Hospital tests showed his colon cancer metastasized and he had "weeks, not months" to live. Without telling him the end was near, I took him home from the hospital. His mind was still sharp; he still had a twinkle in his eye.

With about a week to live, Dad winked at me, saying "why don't you move up to this house?" He knew how much I thought about him. I hoped he realized everything I had done against Carolyn was to protect him. He was still my hero.

We took his ashes up to Fort Rosecrans National Cemetery and put them in the columbarium niche with Mom's ashes. I thought I felt Mom communicating to Dad, "What the hell were you thinking?" as the attendant was replacing the marble face plate.

Our mother Mae would have been proud of Pat and me.

It was now pay-back time for my favorite Internet Whore. I subscribed to the Israeli policy of an eye-for-an-eye.

I called Erv to let him know what part he played in the Carolyn-Frank affair. Erv was astonished at how much I knew about him: the executor of his estate [owner of a near-by Chinese restaurant], the fact he didn't have children, his involvement with Carolyn and Carolyn's long time affair with Erv's friend, retired Love Judge Len. As I went through specifics about Carolyn using him as a pawn to make Dad jealous, Erv asked me, "What's in this for you?"

I replied, "**REVENGE**! That Evil Bitch has destroyed family relationships and it is get-even time, time to hopefully inflict some measure of pain on 'The Biggest Gold Digger in Southern California.'"

Erv listened without comment. He was in his mid-80's and I didn't know how he'd react. Then I told him I would send him a packet of proof. I forwarded many of the documents I had sent to the District Attorney and included damaging emails between Carolyn and Betty, which portrayed Erv as a stooge to make Dad jealous. Just for good measure, I slipped in several pictures of Dad and Carolyn at Dad's house over-looking San Diego Bay.....so Erv would hopefully realize Carolyn was after the expensive house over-looking the harbor, not his house on the Lake.

I called Erv the following week to insure he had received the material. He had, but made no comment. I decided to leave it at that. Since 2000 I had spent far too much time on that despicable scum, Carolyn Smith.

I decided not to go after Retired Love Judge Len Turner even though he deserved it. Enough time had been wasted on low-life predators. It was time to start enjoying retirement instead of wallowing in the pigsty, despite the fact it would still be a kick to screw-over a dishonest judge.

There was a little score, however, to settle with Bruce. Without telling Pat and me, Bruce had obviously gone back on his word we would all stick together against Carolyn. Bruce may have been suckered in by Dad's "I don't want to live any more" campaign, hoping we'd back off opposing Carolyn.

Pat and I had discussed Dad's "threat" when Dad first mentioned it. We thought it was just a ploy to get us to back off; Dad would not commit suicide. Apparently Bruce didn't agree, but he never told us he was switching sides. Carolyn certainly thought so: *"I'll only deal with Bruce."*

Bruce told Dad that Pat and I were monitoring his emails. Dad mentioned this to Pat. Dad also let Pat hear a voice mail recording from Bruce that "Dad should do what he wants regarding Carolyn

Smith." Dad apparently thought this might influence Pat to back down, too. Plus, Bruce had gotten Ken to take a stand against me.

Why? Who knows? With Bruce, it was often difficult to understand "why." As mentioned, his actions were frequently irrational and almost always damaging.

I fired an email off to Bruce, demanding to know why he had knifed us in the back, sabotaging our efforts against Carolyn without telling Pat or me.

He replied with "Fuck you. Kiss my ass."

I hadn't been around my twin much since we were both 18. At this point it looked like I would be spending about as much time with Bruce as I did with Carolyn.

Pat and I had a "Celebration of Life" for Dad at the San Diego Yacht Club. We invited Dad's favorite Yacht Club bar tenders and waiters in addition to his handball buddies and many friends he made while retired in San Diego. I decided to tell humorous stories about Dad's life, including his unbelievable driving close-calls and car ownership stories [he once owned a used Lincoln Town Car he thought was a Cadillac; he could care less about cars, finally drove a Toyota Camry for years because he heard they were the most reliable car]. It didn't make sense to talk about his remarkable life or him as a person. Everyone knew how successful he had been, what a wonderful person he was.

I read nice notes from Mel Laird & the retired Chairman of the Joints Chiefs of Staff plus other well-known people who had worked with Dad. Then I read this email from a friend of mine who had not met Dad:

"I just read the biography of your father's extraordinarily successful life. You must have been a huge disappointment to him."

That was it. The Carolyn Smith Era finally ended with the "wrong" death. I always hoped someone "with nothing to lose" would waste her before Dad died so we could enjoy his final years without worrying about "The Biggest Gold Digger in Southern California."

We were lucky—-and frankly deserving—-of the outcome. I had spent seven all-consuming years of my life to protect Dad from Carolyn Smith. The nightmare had taken a tremendous toll on everyone, forever fracturing family relationships.

She didn't get the $10 Million or kill Dad. I didn't have to body-count Carolyn. Was it worth it?

The first morning I awoke to see the sun rising over San Diego harbor from the house both Richard Nixon and Carolyn Smith wanted but couldn't have, I had my answer. Now I could finally throw away Carolyn's "A.O.L. In Love" picture I had carried in my wallet for almost seven years.

Bye, Bitch!..........this time you really are history............

The SEALS are correct: It pays to be a winner.

With an aging population of seniors like me, we will continue seeing more elder economic exploitation. Dad's situation with Carolyn taught me a lot: I'm currently looking for young, attractive predators [women!] who would like to use their sexual talents in an attempt to wrestle my now-sizeable estate from me. There are limited openings several nights so please book early! Wednesday is amateur night.

Seriously, good luck! And remember, as my Ranger Instructors and Cousin Ronnie kept reminding me:

"DON'T EVER GIVE UP!"

Finally, to my comrades who served in the 101st Parachute Infantry and at Gia Vuc Special Forces Camp, to the memories of Tony Mavroudis, Bob Arvin & my West Point classmates killed in action possessing so much more promising talent than I ever had, and to everyone who has served this wonderful country of ours,

NO SLACK!

2

ELDER FINANCIAL ABUSE: How to stop it

Why is there an Elder Economic Exploitation Epidemic? Like the famous bank robber Willie Sutton said when asked why he robbed banks, "That's where the money is."

Seniors have wealth. Boomers [born 1946-1964] have lots of money. Seniors are often vulnerable targets and poor witnesses, offering predators excellent financial return with little risk or capital. Only a small percentage of Elder Financial Abuse cases are even reported. If Predator is caught and prosecuted, penalties are often light........an unbelievably good business model for Predator.

How do we stop low-life, bottom-feeding parasites from preying on our seniors? The most important lesson I learned over the past ten years: Don't wait for help from anyone; you might as well look up a dead horse's ass. The old saying, "We're from the Government & we're here to help" applies. Yeah, right!

Assume you have to do it yourself or it won't get done. Adult Protective Services, Lawyers, District Attorney for Elder Abuse, Law Enforcement, Trusts, Prenups: again, look up a dead horse's ass!

Elder Financial Abuse laws are weak and favor Predator; why, then, should we expect law enforcement officials to be effective, especially since seniors are often ineffective witnesses against predators? I finally succeeded against the ultimate predator, Carolyn Smith, because it became obvious—-after years—-traditional solutions involving traditional "authorities" wouldn't work. Effective action had to be taken by me.

Our seniors are under attack from an ever-increasing number of parasites: relatives [can you say "Children"], care-givers, retirement home staff, phone scams, charity scams, religious scams, sweetheart scams [Senior Love can strike fear into many a kid's heart]. You name it, if it has chance to separate Senior from his/her money, vultures will try it. Every day some bottom-feeder invents a new scam. One of my favorite targets: variable annuities and other "investment" opportunities for seniors, including reverse mortgages.

In his book "Financial Abuse of the Elderly, A Detective's Case Files of Exploitation Crimes," Joe Roubicek—-during 20 years as a detective investigating Elder Financial Exploitation—-identified one of the most egregious scammers as a Catholic Priest. Another predator was a West Point graduate who used phony medical devices to scam large amounts of money, convincing terminally ill, desperate cancer victims the bogus devices could save them.

In many cases Joe Roubicek investigated, Predator got off scott-free or with very little punishment. The Priest and West Point "ozone therapy" Predator walked away untouched. The Priest got millions in real estate and donations while the West Point "medical expert" received a lot of money from desperate cancer victims, endangering their health even further with his bogus medical procedures. These examples were typical of the cases Joe investigated. Predators know they have an excellent chance of succeeding with very little legal risk.

A common thread through Joe's cases was victimized seniors were almost always isolated from family and friends who could have sensed a rat. When intervention finally occurred, predators had already done serious economic damage.

Predators know they will receive ample warning prior to actual prosecution, permitting Predator to gage how serious the legal threat might be. If a legal warning light starts blinking, Predator simply moves on to the next potential victim. There's an unlimited supply of victims, maybe with even more money. It's a game of high-reward, little risk. Time is the only investment required.

As old age takes its toll on seniors, defensive abilities decline. Seniors can be naively trusting, assuming others—-including Vultures, Parasites & assorted Scum—-are as honest as they are. Short-term memories begin to fail, confusion is more common and loneliness becomes an issue as spouses and friends pass. Seniors become easy targets for unscrupulous predators, especially if the seniors are alone with no protection [you!].

Even if Predator is indicted, Senior can be an ineffective witness, often with a poor memory, embarrassed to testify against Predator.

Trying to protect a senior is often similar to protecting a child. Senior can appear defenseless, unable to process evidence against Predator. Attempts to convince Senior that Predator is only interested in money often fall flat, with the whistle blower designated as a money-grubbing messenger, not someone trying to protect Senior. Aging robs Senior of many intuitive instincts which—-years earlier—-might have caused a red flag to be raised.

Remember: if Senior is mentally competent [knows his/her name, address] and Predator hasn't harmed or stolen from Senior, there is virtually nothing the "authorities" can do to help. It doesn't matter if Predator has just been released from prison after killing a third spouse. Plus, "stolen from Senior" may be VERY difficult to prove.

You can also assume—-if Predator is a pro—-trusts, prenups and Family Limited Partnerships may be of limited value. Pieces of paper won't stop expert parasites, especially if Predator has access to legal advice like Carolyn did. Trusts, prenups, Family Limited Partnerships: they're for honest people, not crooks.

104

Many legal documents intended to protect Senior are primarily for death or divorce. Predator can do serious damage while Senior is just plain living, spending money.

Carolyn would have had no problem getting Dad's stocks, bonds and cash [60-70% of his net worth]. The only "problem" for Carolyn would have been Dad's $3 million house. However, it would have been no problem for a crook. Ex-husbands, Carolyn's relatives and others said Carolyn, once married, would have demanded Dad move out of the area ["too many memories in this house"] so they could start "a new life together." Once the old house was sold, Carolyn could have put the new house in both names or her name.

Moving Dad out of the area would have isolated him from Pat and me so she could have completed her revenge against us, becoming a wealthy woman.

Another lesson learned during my involvement with Carolyn: don't waste time "selling" Senior that Predator doesn't have Senior's best interests in mind. If you are initially unsuccessful convincing Senior that Predator is a con artist, stop "selling" Senior, attack Predator.

How? Let Predator know you're not going to stand by to watch your senior become another victim of Elder Financial Exploitation. Create as much turmoil and havoc as possible. If Predator is selling an un-needed variable annuity and he refuses to stop, go to the parent company, threatening legal action. These companies know they shouldn't be selling variable annuities to seniors, that variable annuities only provide a hefty commission to the sales person without any advantage to Senior.

Don't listen to Senior's threats to mind your own business or there will be financial inheritance retribution. Just do it! Seniors often side with predators, feeling the family member or other protectors are the greedy ones. Senior will quickly forget the matter and won't carry through with any threats. Trust me!

You have to introduce "risk" into Predator's life; you must be creative. What does Predator fear most? Threatening legal action against a company selling unnecessary variable annuities? Going to the Better Business Bureau? Calling the Police? Involving a lawyer? Calling Predator's friends? Involving a Private Detective?

Why am I mentioning lawyers and police if I previously said they wouldn't work? I didn't say not to use them, I said to assume they would not do YOUR job. You can involve attorneys & police and threaten their use to Predator, just don't expect the "authorities" to take effective action against Predator. YOU have to do that!

Act! Do your homework, come up with a plan but don't spend too much time analyzing a plan to death. Acting expeditiously rather than wasting too much time perfecting a plan is key. Often any resistance, regardless how minor, will convince Predator to move on to the next victim.

I am not suggesting you break the law. You should try legal methods first, then decide what's next. I broke many laws and threatened to kill Carolyn because I was convinced she would kill my father. Were my actions correct? My answer is that an evil, dangerous predator wasn't successful against someone I loved very much. Additionally, compare what happened in my case to my spending time in jail for murder. Those were my options: stop the marriage or consider killing Carolyn.

Many predators are cowards or wimps. They want the easy victory, not a hassle. There are too many potential victims to get bogged down with your senior. If you show you're up for a fight, Predator will slither away to search for an easier mark.

What is Elder Economic Exploitation? I define it simply as the misuse of Senior's assets. Joe Roubicek's book does an excellent job outlining the difference between Elder Fraud and Elder Exploitation. However, definitions really aren't important. Basically, Elder Economic Exploitation is the use of Senior's hard-earned money for goods or services Senior that don't benefit Senior.

Instead of complaining about the current legal system or beating your head against the wall to change laws, attack Predator. Don't let the bastard get away with it! Sure it's not fair! Sure it sucks! Sure, laws should protect vulnerable seniors. But your time is better spent getting rid of the problem, not trying to influence something you probably can't change: ineffective Elder Financial Abuse laws.

Some other points:

Insure Senior is not isolated. That's asking for trouble, making Senior an easy mark. Carolyn obtained her town home and Geraldine's assets because Geraldine's only blood relatives—-4 brothers—-had no contact with her. They showed up for the distribution of assets after Geraldine passed only to find Carolyn had gotten everything. Legal recourse against Carolyn wasn't worth the financial risk, according to Geraldine's Brothers' lawyer.

We were successful against Carolyn because we discovered who she was—-a dangerous predator—-7 weeks into the scam. Had Dad been isolated, Carolyn would have spun her black widow web. If Dad married Carolyn, she would have ended up with EVERYTHING, including Dad's early demise. Don't take my word for it, ask Carolyn's relatives........or Geraldine's!

Find out if Senior is wasting money on unnecessary goods or services, including love! Seniors are often lonely. They are willing to waste lots of money on companionship of any type.....from unscrupulous phone-calling sellers of anything to sweet hart scams. Whether it's an un-needed new roof, a variable annuity or love/companionship, find out where Senior is wasting money—-hopefully as early as possible.

In his "Ten tips to help you reduce the risk of becoming the next victim of Financial Elder Abuse," Paul Greenwood, San Diego Deputy District Attorney & Head of Elder Abuse Prosecution, says to "consider allowing your bank to send a duplicate copy of Senior's monthly statement to a trusted family member or professional advisor. Most financial elder abuse cases are only reported or discovered six to nine months after the initial losses have occurred. Elders whose sight is failing are at greater risk because they may rely upon the very person who is stealing from them to insure the financial transactions are in order. An independent pair of eyes that are able to look over bank statements every 30 days will be able to catch suspicious activities in the early stages."

If you control Senior's money and spending, you control Predator.

Find out about Predator. What's his M.O.? What does she fear? Who else has he scammed? Go on the Internet. It's amazing what you can find out about Vultures, Vermin, Parasites and Scum on the Internet. Do your homework.

If you can't find out about Predator's background on the Internet, hire a private investigator. Private Investigators can often be effective and uncover valuable information, although some of the same information may be available to everyone on the Internet [free and for a fee]. A Private Investigator may also help you formulate a plan.

If you don't think it's important to learn the background of potential predators, read Aphrodite Jones' non-fiction book, "Della's Web," where a man-hater with four previous violent marriages used a dating service to con a prominent surgeon into marriage. The surgeon was attracted to the dating service because it was not free, used a system to qualify applicants.

In Aphrodite's acknowledgments, she concluded, "Although Deborah [the murdered Surgeon's daughter] didn't want the book written, she came to see its potential value to all the men and women out there who marry for the wrong reasons. Maybe this story will cause someone out there to think—-to prevent future marriage vows from becoming fatal."

It would have been VERY easy to uncover Della's sordid past, possibly in a couple hours, maybe with a few phone calls—-probably at no cost. It was surprising to me how many red flags came up before the marriage of Della and the Surgeon [and why a friend or relative—-or the Surgeon's lawyer—-didn't take action or suggest to the Surgeon that he obtain a background check on Della]. In my situation with Carolyn, I had far fewer red flags, only suspicions about her "phoniness" and questions about her history. I didn't know if Carolyn was a threat to Dad, I just wanted to find out who she was; all we had was Carolyn's version. Like Ronald Reagan said, "Trust, but verify."

If damage has already been done, see if you can un-do it. Firms selling variable annuities will probably reverse the transaction rather than fight. An un-needed new roof? Raise hell! Get a lawyer to write a letter. Try something, see what happens. Don't let Scum get away with it! Fix bayonets, charge!

Use available resources. Talk to lawyers [whose initial consultation is often free], police, Adult Protective Services, the District Attorney for Elder Abuse, the newspaper columnist, Better Business Bureau, friends, strangers, anyone. Get what you can from the Internet [Google "Elder Financial Abuse/Exploitation;" you'll learn a bunch].

Get a copy of Edward Carnot's book, "Is Your Parent in Good Hands?" Carnot, an attorney, reviews how he tried to protect his father from a greedy caregiver. In addition, Carnot provides an excellent over-view of asset-protection and numerous issues related to senior care. Unfortunately, Carnot's book was not published until after the Carolyn debacle. "Is Your Parent in Good Hands" would have provided valuable guidance, especially regarding the ineffectiveness of Elder Financial Abuse Laws.

All the research and homework—-and involvement with local authorities—-will help you come up with a plan.

Don't stand for it! Finally, you have to act in order to stop vultures from preying on your senior. Make the vultures as miserable as possible. Predators should know, if they're planning to get money from a senior, the money's not coming from your senior......not without a BIG fight!

Some other tips from Paul Greenwood's Top Ten List:

>Choose a caregiver with caution. Do not assume by hiring a caregiver through a bonded agency you are guaranteed to get someone who has been checked.

Many predators want to work as caregivers or in retirement homes since that work puts them in easy reach of their victims. Carolyn worked retirement homes, gaining access to easy prey.

>Don't assume the friendly handyman is in fact licensed. Obtain three estimates in writing and, if you don't know the contractor, check with both the Better Business Bureau and the State License Contractor's Board. DON'T rely on the contractor's impressive business card with a contractor's license number on it. Never pay more than 10% of the contract price up front.

Paul's other Top Ten Tips:

>Keep an inventory of all jewelry

>Every home should have a shredder

>Protect incoming and outgoing mail

>Obtain a credit search on yourself two or three times/year

>Every telephone should have caller I.D. Telephone is a crook's weapon of choice.

>You will NEVER win the Canadian Lottery. Disregard letter from Nigeria or Madrid about receiving a substantial amount of money.

>Always have a second line of defense at your front door

If your initial plan of attack against Predator doesn't work, try something else. Keep your options open. Keep trying until something convinces Predator to move on to his next victim. They will move on, guaranteed. The Cheetah has lots of prey grazing on the Serengeti Plain. Why chase fast animals when there are plenty of older, slower food choices?

Carolyn Smith was the exception. She found a $10 million pay day and decided it was worth the fight. Plus, she had a burning desire to get even with me for the pain and humiliation I inflicted on her. Most scum won't fight that hard. They don't have the guts....or brains. They'll slither out of your life with barely a whimper.

If you work only within the system, using traditional authorities, adhering to the letter of the law, you'll lose. You'll get added "benefits" of becoming exasperated, frustrated and depressed, feeling your hands are tied while Predator enjoys protection of the law.

This was brought home to me in Stephanie Germack's book, "Legal and Financial Exploitation of our Elders." Stephanie's siblings obtained an Involuntary Guardianship over their mother, controlling Mom's finances and dictating her care. Stephanie was unaware of her sibling's initial intentions.

Stephanie only worked within the system, guaranteeing failure [I'm assuming Stephanie's version of the story is correct, which could be the wrong assumption. Her siblings obviously have a much different version]. Stephanie then spent an inordinate amount of time bashing the system and contemplating changing the law.

What should she have done? Assuming the siblings were wrong, Stephanie should have attacked the siblings, not work only within a system which favors the "bad guys."

How?

One strategy could have been to "kidnap" Mom, keep her at Stephanie's house in a different state [from the siblings], which might have forced her siblings to negotiate [instead of Mom going involuntarily into a care facility immediately]. As it worked out, Stephanie had no say in the care of Mom or the disposition of Mom's assets.

Would it have been fair for Stephanie to "kidnap Mom?" Of course not, but her siblings were not fair by blind-siding Stephanie with an Involuntary Guardianship, excluding Stephanie from any decisions affecting the remainder of their Mother's life.

Instead, Stephanie caved into the system, resorting to legal representation and prayer while ultimately working to change the law. Nothing against prayer, but Stephanie violated my key principle: attack the predators. Even if Stephanie could not have avoided Involuntary Guardianship for Mom, at least Stephanie might have forced her siblings to the negotiation table, hopefully resulting in Stephanie having some say in the care & feeding of Mom [and a vote in the use of Mom's considerable assets]. As it turned out, Stephanie was left out in the cold while her siblings had complete control, leaving Stephanie looking up a dead horse's ass to change the law. Yeah, right! Good luck!

You have to become a "street fighter" when dealing with bottom-feeding scum. They know the law. They know the law protects them until proven guilty, which RARELY happens.

Like the Ranger School instructors taught us in the hand-to-hand combat pit: it's one-on-one, no rules. Anything goes. You're not guilty unless you get caught. Even if you get caught, you might face a sympathetic Judge who understands frustration with weak Elder Financial Abuse laws.

Get nasty. Play Predator's game. Don't wait for help from someone else. It's your senior at risk. It's YOUR job to protect Senior, not the DA, APS or some other agency that will leave you frustrated, looking up a dead horse's ass.

Vultures trying to scam Senior's money are nasty, despicable, lo-life parasites. They have no intention of playing fair. Why should you?

Become a street fighter, assume Gunny Sergeant Lee Ermey is your squad leader: "Kick ass, Maggot!"

You'll feel a lot better.

Our seniors spent a life-time earning, saving, investing.....working honestly to provide a decent life for their families. Don't let predators come in during Senior's ninth inning of life to end up with Senior's hard-earned assets, leaving a bitter family legacy.

No Slack......Attack!

3

WHERE ARE THEY NOW? What happened to the main characters in "Kill Mom?"

CAROLYN SMITH: Still practicing her trade of fleecing Seniors. Within the last year she moved into a house on the golf course at the Lake, renting out the town home she conned from Geraldine. Originally the golf course house was put in Love Judge's Len Turner's name, who then transferred ownership to Carolyn. She had to fleece a senior; you don't buy a house on the golf course with social security wages. Tag-team of Carolyn and the Love Judge still going strong.

LOVE JUDGE LEN TURNER: See above. Continuing to barter legal advice for sex with Miss Carolyn. Lovely couple of Scum Bags.

DICK, Carolyn's Son: Lives in Northwest with second wife, young daughter. Still a Dick-Head!

ERV: Carolyn milked him as a stooge to make Frank Bradley [Dad] jealous. Erv continued to help Carolyn financially until his death in 2009 [mid-80's]. Carolyn may have gotten money from Erv to fund her golf course house.

FRED SMITH, Carolyn's Second Husband: Passed away in 2008 while living at the Lake. Fred's son [lives near the Lake] was unable to continue providing intelligence about Carolyn because he hated Carolyn so much for what she did to ruin their father-son relationship.

TIM, Carolyn's Third Husband she met through newspaper personals: Moved to Northern California with wife who talked him out of killing Carolyn. Very happy to be away from Lake area, Carolyn Smith. Also delighted he didn't kill Carolyn because Tim now knows "nothing to lose" didn't apply to him. Carolyn has no idea how close she came to "buying the farm." She can thank Tim's doctors for treating his cancer.

PAT, My Sister: Still lives in Point Loma. Her husband Ken passed away in 2005, so Pat and her three closest friends are now widows. They've replaced husbands with dogs, yielding excellent results [Dogs for Dicks Program]. Apparently wives don't miss us when we check out! For some reason that didn't surprise my wife: "Some women have all the luck!"

BRUCE, My Brother: Lives on East Coast. Pat and I have little contact as a result of his campaign sabotaging our efforts to protect Dad. Elder Economic Exploitation produces considerable collateral damage!

GINNY, Carolyn's Sister: Apparently still lives in Florida; don't know the relationship she has with Carolyn or Carolyn's son Dick as a result of Ginny assisting us.

MYSTERY RELATIVE: I was greatly assisted by one of Carolyn's relatives who I promised not to compromise. This person is a class act who provided excellent intelligence about Carolyn and other unsavory co-conspiring Scum, confirming Carolyn is a dangerous predator only interested in money. I will be forever indebted to this wonderful individual who risked much to help me. Person was instrumental in my decision to take drastic action against Carolyn in order to protect Dad. A true hero! Words can't express my sincere appreciation, probably keeping me out of jail. You know who you are. I wish there were some way I could repay you.

DAD [FRANK BRADLEY]: Sharing a columbarium with Mom at beautiful Rosecrans National Cemetery over-looking San Diego Harbor and the Pacific Ocean. Nice place to visit, not to live.

Dad is still catching it from Mom about his dreadful judgment of picking Carolyn over his own children. Don't worry, Dad, the constructive criticism will only continue for eternity.

ME: Thanks for asking. Considering my low-I.Q., bad judgment and short pecker, doing great. I still have serious mental problems but it beats reality.

MY WIFE: The luckiest woman in the world.

WHERE ARE THEY NOW [Part II]

CAROLYN SMITH: Forgot to mention: she's my Cougar. She's still trying to screw me, but in a good way. Dad was right..........................she's one hell of a woman!

4

FINALLY

I asked ten friends to review my manuscript. They're now ex-friends. Okay, so I'm no Hemmingway or Stephen King, but I majored in Killing, not Journalism or English.

I received great input, critique and suggestions: use a ghost writer, pay an editor, learn how to use Microsoft Word, get proof readers, hire a literary agent........all manner of suggestions to correct my manuscript. Also, "base it on a true story," making it more like a "traditional" book, a novel.

Then I had a brilliant thought: "Fuck it!" Actuarially, I have 127,727 hours remaining before the Big Infantry Guy in the sky calls my dog tag serial number. I got better things to do.

I'm retired; I don't need to be pretending to be an author. Impersonating an author should be a felony, fortunately—for me—it's not. Happily, this book is short enough it won't be cluttering up reader's minds, leaving little space for *Snookie of Jersey Shore*, *Keeping Up with the Kardashians* or *The Bachelorette*.

Finally, it dawned on me: I almost flunked Plebe English before defending our country against hoards of Communist Insurgents after fighting on the Russian Front in Berlin. Without my efforts in Vietnam [we were winning when I left!], buyers of this book would probably be speaking Vietnamese. After all I've done, readers should be able to over-look misspelled words, split infinitives, syntax issues, poor grammar, awkward sentence structure and dangling participles [insensitive comments rudely scribbled on my Plebe term papers].

Good news is I won't have to go on any book signings. On the other hand, Shakespeare never went on any book signings and he did pretty well.

If you want a book signed, bring it to South Beach Bar & Grill in Ocean Beach any lunch time. Food and views are great.

No Slack

Bob Bradley
p.o. Box 6578, San Diego, Ca 92166
bobbradleykm@yahoo.com [also Facebook]
Twitter: BobBradleykm
Phone number: You think I'm crazy!

Made in the USA
San Bernardino, CA
19 March 2015